50¢

SEVEN LEVELS
OF GLORY

*"For the earth will be filled with the knowledge of
the glory of the Lord, as the waters cover the sea."*
(Habakkuk 2:14)

JAMES A. DURHAM

PRESS

Seven Levels of Glory
by James A. Durham

Printed in the United States of America

ISBN 9781626978294

www.xulonpress.com

TABLE OF CONTENTS

—⚬⚬⚬—

ACKNOWLEDGEMENTS

———*ων*———

I want to express my thanks first and foremost to the Lord for providing the revelation for this book and for the inspiration along the way to complete the project. The Lord is good and His love and mercy endure forever. Without Him none of our works would succeed. It is with gratitude and praise that I acknowledge all He has done to make this book possible.

I want to acknowledge the invaluable assistance I received from my extremely blessed, highly favored, and anointed wife, Gloria. Without her encouragement and assistance this book could never have been completed. I am also grateful for her dedicated and tireless assistance in proof reading the book and confirming the accuracy of the scriptural references. I also want to acknowledge my daughter, Michelle, who remains a constant and consistent cheerleader throughout the process of all my writings. Anytime I needed encouragement, I had only to turn to either of these two wonderful ladies. I am so thankful to the Lord that He placed them in my life and constantly blesses me through their love and support!

I would like to express appreciation to many who have encouraged and supported me in the many months required to complete this project. I cannot mention all, but give a special word of gratitude to my good friend Pastor Seong Hyun Beck, Tongyeong Woori Church who first spoke to me about the seven levels of glory.

I am also grateful to the members of King of Kings Church in DaeJeon, Korea, and especially to Pastor (Dr.) Tae-gil Ahn for giving me the opportunity to spend time with them in the presence of His glory. It was in the moments following our meeting with them in the glory presence of the Lord that this revelation came.

You have each been a blessing and inspiration to me and I will always be grateful.

PREFACE

A NEW DIMENSION OF GLORY

During an extended ministry trip to South Korea in October 2012, the Lord gave me an amazing revelation of His glory and the very systematic way in which He has chosen to reveal it to us. Then the Lord began to reveal that He lifts us up into His glory in the same systematic way. The trip to Korea got off to a rough start with canceled flights and mechanical problems. However, the Lord turned these struggles into something very positive by giving us opportunities to minister in His glory in the airports and on the planes. To give you a better understanding of what I mean, I will share some notes about this trip from my journal of these encounters with the Lord.

JOURNAL ENTRY
(Friday Morning, October 12, 2012)

We are finally here (Seoul, South Korea), and it started to feel like home as soon as we entered the city. From the beginning of this journey, we were faced with unexpected delays due to mechanical problems with airplanes, canceled flights, and luggage misplacement. We missed our connection in Chicago and had to spend the night in a hotel. Then we were placed on an older and less comfortable airplane. Our seat assignments were changed and we were seated well apart from one another.

We arrived a day later than planned, and missed our time of rest before the ministry began. But, what the enemy planned for evil the Lord worked for good. At every step along the way, we had divine appointments, and the Lord used the delays for kingdom business. Amen! Thank you Lord!

This morning the presence of the Lord was unusually strong in our hotel room. We were visited by angels as the Holy Spirit ministered to us in spirit, soul, and body. The presence of His glory became too strong to remain standing and I went to my knees before Him. At this point, I went into an open vision in which I saw something like a picture in a frame located a long distance away. I was drawn toward it by the Spirit. As I got closer, I could see that it was shaped like a square frame with a three dimensional, living picture inside.

As I watched, I was drawn into the picture. It was then that I realized that this was actually a portal into Heaven. The Holy Spirit made me aware for the first time that there are Kingdom Portals on the earth just like the ones into Heaven. I remembered something Paul wrote.

"But even to this day, when Moses is read, a veil lies on their heart. Nevertheless when one turns to the Lord, the veil is taken away. Now the Lord is the Spirit; and where the Spirit of the Lord is, there is liberty. But we all, with unveiled face, beholding as in a mirror the glory of the Lord, are being transformed into the same image from glory to glory, just as by the Spirit of the Lord." (2 Corinthians 3:15-18)

This morning, it felt like a veil had been removed from my eyes and I was seeing very clearly into another reality. The Holy Spirit revealed to me that we had moved from one level of glory into another. Our journey in the glory is seldom if ever on the same level as the last one. We are always moving upward to a higher level resulting in more and more opportunities to experience greater intimacy with the Lord. As I reflected on Paul's teaching about going from "glory to glory," I realized that this passage is not just about individuals, but also for the corporate body of Christ as it allows itself to be led by the Holy Spirit.

As I moved through this portal, I saw row after row of mountain ranges cloaked in darkness and surrounded by areas of deep fog. The Lord was teaching me visually that we have been in the "valley of the shadow" (this is what the Spirit called it). Most of us have had some valley experiences in the past few years. Many of you have experienced pain, loss, and hardships which may have felt like times of real tribulation. If you have been through some of these times, pause a moment and think about it! For those who are being led by the Spirit, the Lord was giving some good news this morning. Now is the appointed time for you to move out of the valley and into a new dimension of His glory. I believe that David must have been emerging from a time like this when he wrote Psalm 23.

> *"Yea, though I walk through the valley of the shadow of death, I will fear no evil; for You are with me; Your rod and Your staff, they comfort me. You prepare a table before me in the presence of my enemies; You anoint my head with oil; My cup runs over. Surely goodness and mercy shall follow me all the days of my life; And I will dwell in the house of the Lord forever."* (Psalm 23:4-6)

The Lord was releasing some good news this morning: On the horizon is a new dimension. It is going to be on a higher level of glory than we have thus far experienced. As I looked up, I was given a vision of something which seemed to be in the future, but which is at the same time very close at hand. I saw a kind of manifestation of a great brightness which is stronger than the sun, and it is moving toward us. By revelation, I immediately recognized that the glory of the Lord is coming on a level much stronger than we have known before.

In the last few weeks, the Lord has told me over and over (especially as I gave prophetic words to others) that He is ready to do something so new that we don't yet have the language to describe it. All of the old ways of thinking, seeing, and understanding need to be renewed. The Lord told me that this is why He had instructed me to begin "to impart a renewed mind (see the description in my book entitled, *"Beyond the Ancient Door,"* "Free to Move About the Heavens"). We need to have our minds radically renewed so that we are able to move away from the old ways and move into His new manifestation of glory. Are you ready for it? If you desire to be ready, you need to spend much time in His presence. Allow Him to renew your mind and transform your soul to prepare you for His coming in power and great glory.

At this point, I was lifted up in the Spirit and positioned just under an open portal into Heaven. The portal (like the picture frame) was also four square in shape. I don't remember ever seeing it like this before. Smoke was spilling over the edge of the portal and flowing down like a waterfall over the earth.

The Holy Spirit told me that Heaven is being made ready for the city which is four square to come down to the earth! The Lord is making ready the new Heaven and the new Earth so that He can tabernacle with us. This was the same promise I received on the Feast of Trumpets and on Yom Kippur! It is ready to manifest! Are you ready? I recommend that you do what I did at this point. I read the passage below again and spent time reflecting on it in order to get a deeper understanding of the glory.

> *"Now I saw a new heaven and a new earth, for the first heaven and the first earth had passed away. Also there was no more sea. Then I, John, saw the holy city, New Jerusalem, coming down out of heaven from God, prepared as a bride adorned for her husband. And I heard a loud voice from heaven saying, 'Behold, the tabernacle of God is with men, and He will dwell with them, and*

they shall be His people. God Himself will be with them and be their God. And God will wipe away every tear from their eyes; there shall be no more death, nor sorrow, nor crying. There shall be no more pain, for the former things have passed away.'" (Revelation 21:1-4)

I tried to enter through the portal, but there was such a strong flow of the Lord's anointing flowing down from the opening that I could not go up through it. I am certain that the Lord is releasing this powerful impartation of His glory from Heaven right now. He is doing this in order to prepare us for what He is going to do very soon through a greater release of His glory. Are you ready for Him to renew your mind so that you will be able to flow with Him? Unless we are willing to risk missing out on a powerful move of God, we need to let go of everything that hinders and be prepared to move quickly with Him. The Holy Spirit reminded me of Philippians 3:13-14,

"Brothers, I do not consider myself yet to have taken hold of it. But one thing I do: Forgetting what is behind and straining toward what is ahead, I press on toward the goal to win the prize for which God has called me heavenward in Christ Jesus."

To move into this new season you must let go of everything from the past. You must be especially diligent to let go of un-forgiveness, bitterness, strife, offense, and jealousy. These things cannot move into the new dimension, and their presence in your spirit and soul will hold you back. If you want to move with the Lord let go of everything that hinders. Forget what is behind! Press into what is ahead! We are receiving that upward calling right now.

The Holy Spirit carried me immediately to the throne room without going through the portal. Things were very different today. There was thunder, lightning, rumbling, and shaking in

Heaven. The lightning was either going out from the Father or being drawn to Him. I couldn't really tell which because it was moving at such a tremendous speed. There was darkness all around and the cloud of His glory was everywhere. Everyone in Heaven was silent and face down. The angels of the Lord had moved back away from Him because the power being released was too great to stand near Him. The four living creatures and the twenty four elders had moved back away from this magnificent release of His power. The only one who had not moved was the Lord Jesus!

This was awesome, exciting, and frightening (in a good way) all at the same time. Our God is awesome, all powerful, and filled with a resolve to accomplish His work for His people and His creation. I want to say that I am ready for it, but in all honesty I can't be certain at this point. How about you? I think we have more preparation to go through.

I am reminded of how great the need is for us to renew our minds and how much we need His help and His fire to burn away everything that hinders. I am aware that we need to let go of the old ways and begin to truly be new creations, being made ready for the Bridegroom to come! May we all diligently seek Him in the new season which is beginning to manifest! May we let Him transform us so that we are ready? Amen and Amen!

I am feeling such a powerful anointing of His Glory right now. My entire body is reacting to His presence right here, right now! I pray that as you read these words, you will also be enabled by the Holy Spirit to experience something like I am receiving right now! May the Lord release this awesome anointing to you as you read this! Amen and Amen!

(End of Journal Entry)

CHAPTER 1

INTRODUCTION

—⁊⁊⁊—

THE LORD IS DOING A NEW THING

"Then He who sat on the throne said, "Behold, I make all things new." And He said to me, "Write, for these words are true and faithful." (Revelation 21:5)

The Lord has spoken to me over and over about doing something "NEW" in this season. It will not be like anything we have seen in the past. We will not be able to look at it and say that we recognize it, because it will be completely new. He said that it would be so new that we don't yet have words in our vocabularies to speak about it or describe it! We cannot call it by a name we have used in the past. We will need a new vocabulary just to speak about it and to share it with others. We have only started now to see these new things, and we are constantly amazed by what He is doing!

We have been sharing these words of the Lord with others! When we talk about it, something new begins to manifest. Remember Revelation 19:10, *"For the testimony of Jesus is the spirit of prophecy."* The very unfortunate reality is that in these new outpourings of His glory, many people see it, experience it, shout Hallelujah, and then want to go back to their old ways! It is uncomfortable for many people to walk in something so new, because they like to have a good handle on the things happening to them and around them. We like to fully understand things which we are experiencing so that we can have some control over them. However, we cannot control this move of God. He is doing it and it is awesome. It is totally out of our control, so that no man or woman can glory in it or from it (see 1 Corinthians 1:29-30, "...*that no flesh should glory in His presence*."). All of the glory goes to Him and to Him alone.

One of the first lessons people seem to learn in these outpourings is that there is a very real difference between ministering in the glory and ministering in the anointing! Under the anointing, the Lord allows impartation, healings, gifts, and etc. to flow though a person. The people receiving in this way have to strive for it, and the minister has to labor through it. If you have done this type of ministry, you have probably experienced suddenly feeling exhausted when the anointing lifts. What seemed to be moving by your own strength was actually being done through the Holy Spirit working in and through you. In reality, the Holy Spirit is using your physical body while He does the ministry. When that anointing lifts, the body is exhausted, but you didn't feel that physical drain while the anointing was flowing. You were being replenished by the Spirit as you were releasing things in the ministry. When the anointing lifts, the sudden experience of fatigue can feel almost overwhelming, and you may feel like collapsing. A powerful desire for an extended period of rest is likely to emerge from your spirit.

When you minister in the glory, it is completely different. In the glory, God does it all! Without any human intervention, the Lord is doing healings, miracles, signs and wonders. If you are ministering in the glory, there will be times when you just step aside and wait on the Lord, because you cannot do anything under the weight of His presence. I have often stepped aside and simply said, "Holy Spirit, here I am. If you want me to do anything, just let me know." As I wait, I begin to hear the

Spirit telling me what to do. Sometimes, the Spirit says go to that person and just hold their hand or touch their forehead. As I do this under the leadership of the Holy Spirit, He moves to release something powerful to that person. It isn't from me. I may not even understand what the Lord is doing in those times. I am not striving with them or working to do something. I am just following the Spirit as directed. The Lord does it all, and receives all the glory.

In this type of ministry, we see so many different things happening. People receive inner healing without the work of a deliverance minister. People receive healings and miracles without anyone praying for them or anointing them with oil. In the testimonies which follow these experiences with the glory, we are always amazed by the things the Lord was doing outside of our awareness. In His wisdom, He is doing a mighty work unknown to any other person.

It is amazing to experience these glory outpourings, and when they conclude, I am thankful and ready to close the meetings. However, many people are not ready, because they are expecting something more. They want the new things of the Lord, but they still want the old ways also. People experience all of these amazing things in the glory, and then still want ministry in the anointing. They have received something much greater than the anointing flowing through any man or woman, but still want something they know and understand better. They seem to feel incomplete without going back to the old methods.

Some people even get offended, and say something like, "I came here for the anointing!" They may even demand to receive ministry under the anointing. Most do actually receive an added blessing under the anointing, but many have made the mistake of letting go of what they received in the glory. They want more, but leave with the lesser gift, because they are looking to the man or woman of God rather than seeking the God of the man or woman. I asked the Lord to help me understand why people do this, and He led me to Isaiah 48.

"You have heard these things; look at them all. Will you not admit them? 'From now on I will tell you of new things, of hidden things unknown to you.'" (Isaiah 48:6)

Notice the Lord's question: *"Will you not admit them?"* This is a question which we must all deal with if we are going to minister in the glory. The Lord is most certainly doing new things. These things are happening now! We must get ready to shift with the Lord's movements if we want to flow in the fullness of what He is doing in and through us in this season. We must get hold of the truth spoken through Isaiah so long ago, *"From now on I will tell you of new things, of hidden things unknown to you."*

We are a blessed generation, because the Lord has allowed us to live in this amazing time and has shown us His awesome goodness which is being released in His glory! I hope you have a strong sense of the privilege which is yours to see these things with your own eyes and experience them through all of your senses. However be aware that with great privilege comes great responsibility. If you want to have these things which are flowing in this mighty move of God, you must be willing to let go of the old things which hinder you. Trust that you will then be able to receive these new Spiritual gifts and a fresh anointing to minister in the glory.

For many who are moving in the gifts of the Spirit, there seems to be a resistance to shifting. It is as if they are saying, "We were part of this move of the Lord through the work of the Holy Spirit from the beginning. The former way is still our new thing!" The methods and practices they are clinging to were new then! But, now the Lord is doing another NEW thing! Can you shift again in this new move of the Lord? The Lord is saying, *"I am doing a new thing!"* *"They are created now, and not long ago; you have not heard of them before today. So you cannot say, 'Yes, I knew of them.'"* (Isaiah 48:7)

What will you do? Will you follow the Lord in these new things or will you hold on to the past? Each of us must answer

16

these questions for ourselves. Not many are ready to operate in the Lord's NEW THING! I believe that there are several reasons why people respond this way. First, many are afraid of what they don't know or understand. This spirit of fear blocks them from receiving what the Lord wants to release to them. Remember 2 Timothy 1:7, *"For God has not given us a spirit of fear, but of power and of love and of a sound mind."* Break free from fear and open the door for His glory to come in! You will be glad you did!

Another reason why some people are hesitant is that they are simply unsure about the results! They like the tried and true things of the past. They know what they will get when they do certain things. However, there is no real certainty in our programs and procedures. Our certainty is in the Lord, and we can trust that His new things will provide for every need and every desire of our hearts. If you are struggling in this area remember what Paul said to Timothy,

"Command those who are rich in this present age not to be haughty, nor to trust in uncertain riches but in the living God, who gives us richly all things to enjoy. Let them do good, that they be rich in good works, ready to give, willing to share, storing up for themselves a good foundation for the time to come, that they may lay hold on eternal life." (1 Timothy 6:17-19)

The real danger is for us to let the rebellious spirit residing in us arise! Most people do not like to hear this. They do not want to admit that they have even a tiny bit of a rebellious nature. However, the fact is that there is some of the rebellious spirit in all of us. One of our key tasks in our walk with the Lord is to take control over this temptation. From early childhood you can see it operating in others. As children play, they are enmeshed in a constant struggle to see who is in charge. In the counseling room, you can see this operating in virtually every marital conflict. Some family therapy theorists hold the belief that this is the central struggle in every relationship. They say that all other presenting problems have all emerged from this struggle for control. We can see it at play in the politics of our nations as people position themselves to be free from restraints and to take control of others.

> "...*then the Lord knows how to deliver the godly out of temptations and to reserve the unjust under punishment for the day of judgment, and especially those who walk according to the flesh in the lust of uncleanness and despise authority. They are presumptuous, self-willed.*" (2 Peter 2:9-10a)

Have you ever found yourself despising authority? Have you ever criticized the leaders of your nation, state, or community? Have you ever wanted to be set free from some of the rules and laws established as a control over the behavior of the citizens of your own homeland? If you answered "Yes" to any of these questions, you have touched on the rebellious spirit in your own soul. When this spirit gets out of control, all manner of evil will be let loose. Through the prophet Isaiah, the Lord spoke to the end result of such behavior.

> "*You have neither heard nor understood; from of old your ears have not been open. Well do I know how treacherous you are; you were called a rebel from birth.* (Isaiah 48:8)

When this spirit is allowed to push us to the extreme, we rebel against God and resist the flow of His glory in our midst. Do you want the glory of God? Then you must deal with your own nature and seek the Lord's help to overcome in all these areas. If you want the glory of the Lord to manifest in your life and ministry, you must put aside all self-seeking and just let Him be in charge. Anything less will hinder the flow of the Spirit, and limit your ability to create an environment which attracts the glory. Jesus warned us! Peter warned us! Paul warned us! Isaiah warned us!

The Lord has spoken to me over and over, "I will not share my glory with another! Remember what He spoke through the prophet Isaiah, *"For my own sake, for my own sake, I do this. How can I let myself be defamed? I will not yield my glory to another."* (Isaiah 48:11) As you respond to this word, remember what I said earlier. My own experience has been that people say "Amen," and then go right back to seeking the anointing of a man or woman!

As I shared this earlier in a conference with pastors and leaders, I received a strong challenge from one person who felt very offended that I was not properly honoring the role of "the anointing" in ministry. I hope that what I am saying will not offend you. When we get into offense and conflict over our theological opinions, we open the door for the enemy to enter and hinder the flow of the Spirit. Strife in the body of Christ grieves the Holy Spirit. We need to rise above offense and separate ourselves completely to the Lord. Remember the teaching in Hebrews 12:14, *"Make every effort to live in peace with everyone and to be holy; without holiness no one will see the Lord."*

I assure you that I do not have any desire to downplay the role of "the anointing" in ministry. I personally minister this way as often as possible. However, when the glory presence of the Lord appears, I step back and relinquish my place to Him. In the absence of the glory, the anointing is a powerful way for us to minister to others. I also want to make it clear that at times The Lord says, "Now, minister in the anointing!" However, I am experiencing Him saying more and more often, "Now, minister in My glory!"

The strongest desire of my heart is to walk in greater intimacy with Him. I am seeking Him with all my heart and trusting Him to do as He has promised. *"You will seek me and find me when you seek me with all your heart."* (Jeremiah 29:13) More and more, I find myself just focused on Him and wanting to feel His presence and hear His voice. I am passionate about seeking Him and I am willing to let go of everything which might hinder that from happening. How about you? Do you desire Him above all else? Are you seeking His face with all your heart?

I believe that we are finally at the place and in the appointed time to see the fulfillment of many Biblical prophecies and promises. I believe that our generation can be called "the generation of Jacob." Remember the Word of the Lord in Psalm 24:6, *"This is Jacob, the generation of those who seek Him, Who seek Your face."* The revelation I received from the Lord is that He is manifesting Himself by drawing near to us in seven stages. I call this move of the Lord, "Seven levels of Glory."

SEVEN LEVELS OF GLORY

The Bible reveals seven levels of God's glory coming down to mankind. In one sense we can look at this as a historical review of how He has revealed Himself to the world. At the same time, this revelation of the progression of His glory also speaks of how He works in each of us individually. We go through all these phases in our evolving relationship with Him. In the same way He has revealed Himself and all of His amazing attributes to humanity, He works in us to make it real in our experience of Him.

Each level brings us into a deepening experience of Him. Each level gives us an ever deepening opportunity for intimacy with Him. Another amazing thing I received by revelation is that within the seventh level there are many other levels. It is in this level that we experience what Paul referred to in 2 Corinthians 3:18,

"But we all, with unveiled face, beholding as in a mirror the glory of the Lord, are being transformed into the

same image from glory to glory, just as by the Spirit of the Lord."

What I learned from spending time with the Holy Spirit is that as we go through our spiritual journey in the glory, two different things will be at work in us. We will experience Him coming down through seven levels as He draws closer to us. Then we will experience ourselves being lifted up through seven levels of glory into His presence – into "the same image". He comes down seven levels in order to initiate the process of lifting us up through seven levels of increasing intimacy with Him.

I am excited about this journey and look forward to experiencing more and more of His amazing glory along the way. This may be a little bit too much for some to assimilate at this point. So, my plan is to take you step by step through these stages of glory in the chapters which follow. In the next seven chapters, I will present what I received from the Lord about how He has chosen to come down to us in order to reveal His nature and His plan for our lives. The final seven chapters will deal with the stages in which we are being lifted up into greater and greater experiences of His glory.

It should go without saying that you may not personally experience these stages in the exact order in which they are presented. The Lord didn't use a cookie cutter to create us and He doesn't relate to us as if we are all alike. He works with each of us in a unique way which will best facilitate our development in the glory. Please do not get mentally tangled up by the order I am using. Always seek your own revelation from the Lord and listen to the Spirit of truth as He speaks to you. I simply hope this book will help you along the way on your journey into the glory of God. Don't let anything hinder you on your journey! Amen?

PRAYER

"Jesus spoke these words, lifted up His eyes to heaven, and said: "Father, the hour has come. Glorify Your Son, that Your Son also may glorify You, as You have given Him authority over all flesh, that He should give eternal life to as many as You have given Him. And this is eternal life, that they may know You, the only true God, and Jesus Christ whom You have sent. I have glorified You on the earth. I have finished the work which You have given Me to do. And now, O Father, glorify Me together with Yourself, with the glory which I had with You before the world was." (John 17:1-5)

PAUSE AND REFLECT ON THESE
SELAH QUESIONS

1. Describe one of your experiences in the manifestation of His glory.

2. What have you done to prepare yourself for this new move of the Lord?

3. What other things do you need to be doing to fully experience His glory?

4. If you have detected any of the rebellious spirit in your heart, what do you plan to do to free yourself from it?

5. How open are you to new revelations from the Lord?

6. Do you need the Holy Spirit to help you open up to the glory? If so, all you need to do is ask!

7. What are you doing right now to seek His face and His glory?

CHAPTER 2

LEVEL 1: GLORY ON THE MOUNTAIN

———⟨∞⟩———

H ave you ever had a mountain top experience? Most people can remember a time when something so significant happened that it became a life-changing experience for them. Many of these events occurred far from an actual mountain. Yet, these kinds of encounters with the Lord are often referred to as mountain top experiences. Have you ever wondered why we use this imagery? Perhaps it originated in the story of Moses encountering God in a burning bush on the top of Mount Horeb which was also known as the "mountain of God" (Exodus 3:1). The meeting which occurred on this mountain changed Moses' life forever, and it also initiated something which would change the history of Israel and impact the entire world.

> "*So when the Lord saw that he turned aside to look, God called to him from the midst of the bush and said, 'Moses, Moses!' And he said, 'Here I am.' Then He said, 'Do not draw near this place. Take your sandals off your feet, for the place where you stand is holy ground.'*" (Exodus 3:4-5)

This was the first recorded Glory manifestation in human history. Of course we know that the Lord met with Abraham many times. *"And the Scripture was fulfilled which says, "Abraham believed God, and it was accounted to him for righteousness." And he was called the friend of God."* (James 2:23) However, the Lord did not reveal the fullness of His glory to the man He called His friend. This honor was reserved for Moses who would demonstrate an entirely different form of relationship with the Creator God of the Universe. The Lord met and talked face to face with Moses in a different way than He had ever done in the past.

When the Lord met with Moses on Mount Horeb, a powerful manifestation of His Glory came down on the mountain. This was truly a history changing event. This first appearance of the fullness of His Glory was only seen and experienced by one man. This fact in no way diminishes the importance of this event, because it marked the beginning of an entirely new and ever growing series of experiences between God and humanity. Unfortunately, we have a tendency to read over this account too quickly because we believe we already know it all. Many older Americans have very clear mental images of this encounter because of a history making movie "The Ten Commandments." Most of those who saw it know the story of Moses' meeting with God more from the movie than from the Bible.

Just as God's manifestation to Moses changed human history, the making of this movie changed the entertainment industry by setting entirely new standards for film graphics. One powerful scene in the movie was designed to portray God's supernatural visitation and calling of Moses to lead the people of Israel out of bondage in Egypt. The world was amazed to see a fire that burned in a bush without consuming it, a whirling cloud of God's presence by day, a fiery column of fire by night and the parting of the Red Sea. Then movie goers around the world gasped in surprise to hear the audible voice of the invisible God speaking to the character portraying Moses. In a bit of movie making irony, Charlton Heston, the actor playing the part of Moses, was also

attributes to Moses and the people. The Lord allowed sinful human beings to meet face to face with a holy God and live. No one thought this was actually possible. They began to see and know that He is merciful and gracious. Step by step He led them into a deeper understanding of His nature and the way in which He relates with His people. First, He reveals himself in Exodus 3:2 as the "Angel of the Lord" (usually understood to be the pre-incarnate Jesus Christ). Then in Exodus 3:4, He is referred to as Adonai (Lord). Then finally, in Exodus 3:14, The Lord tells Moses that He is the great "I AM."

> *"And God said to Moses*, "I AM WHO I AM." *And He said, "Thus you shall say to the children of Israel*, 'I AM has sent me to you.'" *Moreover God said to Moses, "Thus you shall say to the children of Israel: 'The Lord God of your fathers, the God of Abraham, the God of Isaac, and the God of Jacob, has sent me to you. This is My name forever, and this is My memorial to all generations."* (Exodus 3:14-15)

Here is an interesting side note. The Lord gives Gideon an almost identical progressive revelation of who He is. In Judges chapter six, verse elevn, He appears as the angel of the Lord. Then in verse fourteen, it is the Lord (Adonai) who is speaking to Gideon. In verse eighteen, the Lord declares His name as "I AM." Finally, in verse twenty, it is once again the angel of the Lord who is speaking to Gideon. You can study this progressive revelation of the Lord to Gideon in Judges 6:11ff. I recommend the use of the "One New Man Bible" for this study because it clearly presents words translated directly from the Hebrew language. Another parallel process of this progressive revelation of the Lord is found in Joshua 5:13-6:5."

Moses only got a glimpse of God's nature, character, and attributes on Mount Horeb. He learned more and more about Him as the Lord continued to speak to him during his negotiations with Pharaoh. However, the next really major manifestation came on another mountain top where Moses literally stepped into the most powerful glory appearance of the Lord in human history. On this mountain Moses began to understand that the Lord was giving him a progressive revelation. When he met with the Lord God on Mount Sinai, Moses received a more complete picture of who God is than when he met with Him on Mount Horeb. Think about that for your own relationship with the Lord. The more time you spend with Him the better you will know Him and the deeper your relationship will grow.

AN UNTOUCHABLE MANIFESTATION
OF HIS GLORY

The Lord really knows how to get your attention. When He appears, it is not just business as usual. You cannot ignore Him or escape from what He is about to do. You can't pretend that nothing is happening when the earth beneath your feet is shaking and quaking. You can't ignore the trumpet blast, the thunder, the lightning, and the fire of God which manifests when He comes into your midst. This is how the Lord came down on Mount Sinai in the sight and hearing of the people of Israel. Fear swept through their midst, and their legs became like jelly and their knees almost rattled with trembling. The people knew that unless the Lord called them up the mountain, anyone who merely touched it would die.

> *"You shall set bounds for the people all around, saying, 'Take heed to yourselves that you do not go up to the mountain or touch its base. Whoever touches the mountain shall surely be put to death. Not a hand shall touch him, but he shall surely be stoned or shot with an arrow; whether man or beast, he shall not live.' When the trumpet sounds long, they shall come near the mountain."*
> (Exodus 19:12-13)

Try to experience this in your own spirit and soul. People today are so casual about authority and many are very emotionally distant from understanding the Biblical concept of "the fear of the Lord." This is a good point to look again at Proverbs 1:7, *"The fear of the Lord is the beginning of knowledge, but fools despise wisdom and instruction."* The importance of understanding the phrase, "fear of the Lord," is made clear by the twenty seven times it appears in the New King James Version of the Bible. As with the people standing at the foot of Mount Sinai, we must learn to deeply respect and highly honor the Lord of lords and King of kings. If you want to experience His glory, show Him that you have this Biblical kind of "fear of the Lord" and that you will always honor and respect Him. If you want a manifestation of His Holy Presence, then establish an atmosphere which welcomes and glorifies Him.

Try to experience what Moses and the children of Israel encountered in this very powerful manifestation of His glory. Close your eyes and try to visualize it! Picture the scene as a cloud descends on the mountain. See the lightning, fire and smoke. Listen in your spirit to hear the sound of violent thundering and the bone chilling sound of a mighty trumpet blast. Feel the ground shaking and see the loose stones on the mountain begin to roll down every incline. Hear the fearful cries of the people around you as you try to avoid getting caught up in their inappropriate spirit of fear. Then suddenly the voice of the Lord breaks through with great power and command authority calling you to come to the mountain. This was no small thing or insignificant event. This appearance of the Lord was about to change human history and start a process of restoring relationships which had been lost since the fall of man in the Garden of Eden. The truth is that each of us needs to come to the mountain of the Lord and see His glory in order to begin our own journey of reconciliation.

"Now the glory of the Lord rested on Mount Sinai, and the cloud covered it six days. And on the seventh day He called to Moses out of the midst of the cloud. The sight of the glory of the Lord was like a consuming fire on the top of the mountain in the eyes of the children of Israel. So Moses went into the midst of the cloud and went up into the mountain. And Moses was on the mountain forty days and forty nights." (Exodus 24:16-18)

No wonder the people thought that Moses was probably dead on the mountain. With their own eyes they had seen the consuming fire resting on the top of the mountain. With their own eyes they had seen Moses courageously walk into the cloud and the fire. Now, it had been forty days since they last saw him or heard from him. What would you have thought if you didn't already know the outcome of this story? If you don't put yourself into this picture, it is easy to look down on them and think that they were foolish to give up so soon. But, would you and I have responded any better than they did? Probably not! Hopefully, we would not resort to idolatry, but we would probably be thinking some of the same thoughts about the fate of Moses. After all, who could possibly survive forty days without food and water in the midst of a consuming fire?

Thank God that Moses went up on the mountain! Thank God that Moses obeyed the Lord and followed precisely what he had been told to do! Thank God that Moses spent forty days in the Lord's presence and brought back this powerful revelation of Who He truly is and what He really expects of us! On Mount Sinai, the Lord gave Moses His most complete self-revelation to this point in human history. From this meeting, we can learn so much about the attributes of the Lord and about what He has planned for us! This moment in revelation history was about to change the worldview of an entire nation and eventually that of the whole planet.

A REVELATION OF HIS GLORY

In this manifestation of His presence, the Lord gave Moses a deeper understanding of His glory than that which had been given to Abraham, Isaac and Jacob. Yet, as awesome and revolutionary as it was, it was still a limited manifestation of God's glory. This was only the first step in a long history of the Lord's sevenfold process of letting us see, understand, and experience His glory. We begin our spiritual journey into the glory at this point, but we are looking forward to something much greater and more powerful than this. In the passage below, try to see yourself having this experience on the mountain and attempt to understand what the writer of Hebrews is trying to say to you in and for this present generation.

> *"For you have not come to the mountain that may be touched and that burned with fire, and to blackness and darkness and tempest, and the sound of a trumpet and the voice of words, so that those who heard it begged that the word should not be spoken to them anymore. (For they could not endure what was commanded: "And if so much as a beast touches the mountain, it shall be stoned or shot with an arrow." And so terrifying was the sight that Moses said, "I am exceedingly afraid and trembling.") But you have come to Mount Zion and to the city of the living God, the heavenly Jerusalem, to an innumerable company of angels, to the general assembly and church of the firstborn who are registered in heaven, to God the Judge of all, to the spirits of just men made perfect, to Jesus the Mediator of the new covenant, and to the blood of sprinkling that speaks better things than that of Abel."* (Hebrews 12:18-24)

In this limited manifestation on Mount Sinai, the Lord came down in His glory, but only to the Mountain Top. He didn't come down the mountain and into the midst of the people at this point. Something important had to be done first to make this possible. If He had manifested His glory in the midst of their sin and uncleanness, most of them would have died immediately. Before they could experience His presence in the camp, they needed to prepare themselves and prepare a holy place for Him to dwell. As you study the scriptures, notice that even when He finally came down into their camp, it was still a limited manifestation of His glory. This is made clear to us in the fact that they were not allowed to enter the tabernacle of His presence.

Only Moses was allowed to go up in this first manifestation of the glory of God. Only Moses had been made clean and holy in His previous and more limited encounters with the Lord. The Lord had established a very special and personal relationship with Moses. *"So the Lord spoke to Moses face to face, as a man speaks to his friend."* (Exodus 33:11a) The people of that time would stand in the doorway of their tents and watch Moses approach God. They didn't venture out to risk life and limb when the cloud of God's presence came down and rested on the tent. They had a limited understanding of the Lord and His nature. It was much easier and safer to just send Moses into the fiery presence of the Lord, and wait for him to return with the Word of God.

As you study these passages of scripture, take note that the manifestation of God's glory on Mount Sinai was also a progressive revelation. Step by step, the Lord began to prepare the people to come into His presence. One of the first persons to be welcomed into His presence was Moses' brother Aaron, the priest. It is important to note here how the Lord works. There is a powerful revelation of the grace and mercy of the Lord in this invitation for Aaron to come into the glory presence of the Lord. This happened after that terrible sin of idol worship at the foot of the mountain. Aaron had made the golden calf and told the people to worship it as the god who brought them out of Egypt. After the Lord's cleansing of his sin, Aaron is invited up the mountain to meet with Almighty God. As he is now welcomed into the Lord's presence, we see that the Lord has forgiven him and restored him. In the invitation given to Aaron, we can see the fullness of the Lord's covering of our sin so that we too can enter into His presence.

"Then the Lord said to him, "Away! Get down and then come up, you and Aaron with you. But do not let the priests and the people break through to come up to the Lord, lest He break out against them." (Exodus 19:24)

The Lord gave Moses a detailed plan for preparing and consecrating Aaron and his sons to minister to Him in the Tabernacle. The Lord also gave Moses the plan for preparing all of the people to meet with Him. *"And Moses took the blood, sprinkled it on the people, and said, 'This is the blood of the covenant which the Lord has made with you according to all these words.'"* (Exodus 24:8) As the old evangelists would say, "Think about it!" It is still the covering of blood which prepares us to enter His presence. In this present generation, it is by the blood of Jesus that we are covered and our sinful hearts are cleansed so that we can draw near to Him.

As you study these Biblical accounts of more and more people being invited into the presence of the Lord, you are given another powerful revelation about our awesome Father God. It is the very nature of the Lord to forgive you and restore you so that you can enter into His presence. This is good news indeed. As this manifestation of the glory continues to progress, others are invited up to the mountain to meet with the Lord. The invitation into His presence moved from Moses to Aaron, to Aaron's sons, and then to some of the leaders of the people.

"Then Moses went up, also Aaron, Nadab, and Abihu, and seventy of the elders of Israel, and they saw the God of Israel. And there was under His feet as it were a paved

work of sapphire stone, and it was like the very heavens in its clarity. But on the nobles of the children of Israel He did not lay His hand. So they saw God, and they ate and drank." (Exodus 24:9-11)

As I studied this passage, I noticed that the writer seemed genuinely surprised that the leaders of the people survived their encounter with the living God. The evidence of their survival was that they were even able to eat and drink after being in His presence. This was as far as this first level of glory was to go. The Lord did not allow the people to come up the mountain. They were still not ready in spirit and soul to encounter the glory of Almighty God. For this reason, the Lord had instructed Moses to keep the general population from coming up with the leaders. The people were greatly relieved by these instructions. They too realized that they were not yet ready to enter the fire of His glory.

"Now He said to Moses, 'Come up to the Lord, you and Aaron, Nadab and Abihu, and seventy of the elders of Israel, and worship from afar. And Moses alone shall come near the Lord, but they shall not come near; nor shall the people go up with him.' So Moses came and told the people all the words of the Lord and all the judgments. And all the people answered with one voice and said, 'All the words which the Lord has said we will do.'" (Exodus 24:1-2)

Did you notice that they answered with "one voice." They were very happy to stay at the bottom of the mountain were it seemed to be safe. In their response, we see the tragic consequences of the wrong kind of fear of the Lord. Inappropriate fear of the Lord keeps us away from his presence and we miss all the wondrous things the Lord releases in His glory. The Biblical type of "the fear of the Lord" is meant to draw us closer to Him. The children of Israel saw their sinfulness, but had not yet appropriated God's covering for their sin. You can only go into His presence if you are wearing His robe of righteousness, His blood covering, and the garment of praise He gives you. Aaron's two oldest sons learned this the hard way.

> *"Then Nadab and Abihu, the sons of Aaron, each took his censer and put fire in it, put incense on it, and offered profane fire before the Lord, which He had not commanded them. So fire went out from the Lord and devoured them, and they died before the Lord. And Moses said to Aaron, 'This is what the Lord spoke, saying: "By those who come near Me I must be regarded as holy; And before all the people I must be glorified."'" So Aaron held his peace."* (Leviticus 10:1-3)

Perhaps you have asked a question I once asked in the past. If the Lord wants us to come into His presence, why would He do this to two of Aaron's four sons? This happened because everyone needs to understand a powerful lesson from their experience. Even though we are invited into His presence, we must still respect His holiness! We must still draw near with deep respect and an appropriate attitude of "the fear of the Lord." Evidently Aaron's two sons failed to do this. First, we see that they offered the wrong kind of fire. They did it the pagan way. They were not obedient to the specific commands of the Lord. If they had gotten away with this major breach in obedience, it would have established a very poor model for the people to follow. I believe that the Lord made it clear what really happened spiritually when Nadab and Abihu died in the fire. Aaron's sons were drunk, disorderly, and disobedient in the presence of the Lord. This is revealed by the Lord's words of correction given to Aaron immediately following this incident.

> *"Then the Lord spoke to Aaron, saying: 'Do not drink wine or intoxicating drink, you, nor your sons with you, when*

36

you go into the tabernacle of meeting, lest you die. It shall be a statute forever throughout your generations, that you may distinguish between holy and unholy, and between unclean and clean, and that you may teach the children of Israel all the statutes which the Lord has spoken to them by the hand of Moses.'" (Leviticus 10:8-11)

THE TORAH WAS GIVEN

I spent a great deal of time meditating and praying about this section of the book. I have a great desire to communicate to you the depth of what the Lord has revealed about the Torah. At the same time, I know that this is a very difficult task. Most Christians have a very limited understanding of the concept of Torah. Very few courses have been offered until recently to enlighten them about this key concept for understanding God's revelation of Himself. My hope and desire is that this study will give you a hunger to learn much more than I am able to cover in this short space.

"Then the LORD said to Moses, "Come up to Me on the mountain and be there; and I will give you tablets of stone, and the law and commandments which I have written, that you may teach them." (Exodus 24:12)

A major confusion seems to exist about this powerful revelation because of an error made by early translators. They used the word "law" as a literal translation of the word "Torah." This is unfortunate because law is a very inadequate word to describe this key Biblical concept. Misconceptions about Torah are further exacerbated when people try to apply the New Testament concept of being set free from the "Law." Some people have gone so far as to suggest that we no longer have any need for the Old Testament. This doctrine has been pushed far beyond anything Jesus or Paul intended and so much of the richness of God's revelation has been neglected. I encourage you to study what Jesus said about this and let the Word of God speak for itself.

> *"For assuredly, I say to you, till heaven and earth pass away, one jot or one tittle will by no means pass from the law till all is fulfilled. Whoever therefore breaks one of the least of these commandments, and teaches men so, shall be called least in the kingdom of heaven; but whoever does and teaches them, he shall be called great in the kingdom of heaven. For I say to you, that unless your righteousness exceeds the righteousness of the scribes and Pharisees, you will by no means enter the kingdom of heaven."* (Matthew 5:18-20)

The Torah is so much more than just commandments and sacrificial procedures. It is the Lord's powerful revelation of who He is and what He expects of us. The word Torah appears more than two hundred times in the original Hebrew text of the Old Testament. The Greek word "Nomos" was used as a translation for the Hebrew word Torah and appears more than two hundred times in the Greek New Testament. There is no equivalent English word for either Torah or Nomos. Most of those translating the scriptures into English simply substituted the word law for both words. However the word "teachings" is a much better translation of the full meaning of Torah. Torah has also been used as a title for the first five books of the Bible. In this usage, we see more of the fullness of its meaning. It incorporates the entire revelation given to Moses of who God is and what He desires for us to be. Many of the Psalms can help you gain a greater understanding of the concept of Torah. Study the two passages below to increase your grasp of the concept of Torah.

> *"The law (Torah) of the Lord is perfect, converting the soul;*
> *The testimony of the Lord is sure, making wise the simple;*
> *The statutes of the Lord are right, rejoicing the heart;*

The <u>commandment</u> of the Lord is pure, enlightening the eyes; The <u>fear of the Lord</u> is clean, enduring forever; The <u>judgments</u> of the Lord are true and righteous altogether. More to be desired are they than gold, Yea, than much fine gold; Sweeter also than honey and the honeycomb. Moreover by them your servant is warned, and in keeping them there is great reward." (Psalm 19:7-11)

"Blessed are You, O Lord! Teach me Your <u>statutes</u>. With my lips I have declared all the <u>judgments</u> of Your mouth. I have rejoiced in the way of Your testimonies, as much as in all riches. I will meditate on Your <u>precepts</u>, and contemplate Your <u>ways</u>. I will delight myself in Your <u>statutes</u>; I will not forget <u>Your word</u>." (Psalm 119:12-16)

Notice the key words used in these two passages to inform your understanding of Torah. It has to do with testimonies, commandments, judgments, statutes, precepts, ways, and His Word. Torah is all of this and more. When you study the Word, put the word Torah back into the scriptures each time you see the word law. It will give you a much more complete understanding of the Word of God when you are able to make this substitution. Reflecting back on what Jesus said about the law (Matthew 5:18-20) substitute the word Torah for Law, and you will have a much better grasp of what He really meant. The nature of God and His desire for us will never change. It will not go away until every prophecy of the Bible has been fulfilled. What the Lord expects of you is changeless. The sacrificial law was fulfilled and we no longer sacrifice animals to atone for sin. Jesus did that once and for all through the sacrifice of His life and the shedding of His blood on the cross. This does not change the fact that the Torah is still in effect today. We must still study the scriptures to understand what the Lord expects of us and how He blesses those who obey Him. With this understanding, reflect on what Paul meant when he wrote:

"All Scripture is given by inspiration of God, and is profitable for doctrine, for reproof, for correction, for instruction in righteousness, that the man of God may be complete, thoroughly equipped for every good work." (2 Timothy 3:16-17)

I believe that understanding more fully the major concepts in the Torah is the key to being enabled to better host His glory. When the Lord placed it on my heart to write this book, I understood immediately that I needed to get deeper into the Torah to complete the task. The detailed accounts of the manifestation of His glory, revealed in the Torah, provide the solid foundation upon which we are to build the rest of our understanding of how to host His presence. Each of us needs to have a Mount Sinai experience with the Lord to begin our journey into the glory. Each of us needs to grasp more fully the nature of our awesome Father God. We need to constantly increase our understanding of His attributes, His plans and purposes for our lives, and how much He desires to tabernacle with us. All of these steps open the way for His glory to reside in us, and be manifest in all of our lives, our families, and our ministries.

WHO HE IS AND WHAT HE DOES

The Lord revealed so much of Himself to Moses, Aaron, Aaron's sons, and the seventy leaders on Mount Sinai. He spoke about His attributes, and then clearly manifested them before the people. Even though He appeared in a cloud, He came down to clear away the fog in our understanding of Him. He wanted you and I to see more and more clearly who He is, what He does, and what He desires for us to be and to do. Too many Christians today have lost touch with the Mount Sinai manifestation. Too many have put aside the teachings of the Old Testament because they were not taught correctly about the meaning of Torah. Now, is the time for that to change as His glory is once again being revealed to us. Now is the time to open our hearts and minds so that the Lord can make these things known once again. Now is the time for Him to manifest Himself in each of our lives, and answer anew the question: Who is this awesome and holy God?

He is the great "I AM!" This is the creator God who spoke to Jacob and said, "I am the God of your father." There are two Hebrew forms of "I AM" used in the Bible. The first and most basic is "Ani." The more powerful and purposeful word "Anokhi" is formed by adding the syllable "khi" to the basic form of the word. When the Lord proclaims "I AM" using this form of the Hebrew word, it proclaims to the listener that what He is saying is accompanied by His power and His purpose. This is the form of the word used by the Lord when He is instructing Jacob to go down to Egypt. In the passage below, notice that the Lord is pointing out that He is the God of Jacob's ancestors. The Lord's intent is clear. He also wants to be the God of Jacob. He wants to fill Jacob's life with power and purpose as He works to establish the destiny of the Hebrew people.

"So He said, "I am God, the God of your father; do not fear to go down to Egypt, for I will make of you a great nation there. I will go down with you to Egypt, and I will also surely bring you up again; and Joseph will put his hand on your eyes." (Genesis 46:3-4), "

Compare this to the Lord's message to Moses on Mount Horeb. In this first encounter with the glory of God, Moses is told, "I am that I am." In other words, the Lord is saying to Moses "I am your God." I am sending you on a great mission, and I plan to release my purpose and power into your life and service. To the people He is still the God of their fathers – the God of Abraham, Isaac, and Jacob. He is the God who has given them a destiny based on His purpose and power. He has given them blessing and favor which is based on their relationship to their ancestors. But to Moses, He is more! His purpose for

Moses includes a lifetime of face to face meetings which will guide the remainder of Moses' time on earth.

> *"God said to Moses, 'I AM WHO I AM. This is what you are to say to the Israelites: "'I AM has sent me to you.'" God also said to Moses, 'Say to the Israelites, "'The LORD, the God of your fathers—the God of Abraham, the God of Isaac and the God of Jacob—has sent me to you.'" This is my name forever, the name by which I am to be remembered from generation to generation.'"*
> (Exodus 3:14-15, NIV)

On the mountain, the Lord also revealed how He wanted His people to live. He wanted them to live in freedom in the land of promise. He wanted to establish them as a holy nation—a kingdom of priests and kings. He wanted them to know that His eyes were on them, He knew what they needed, and He had compassion on them. His purpose for them went far beyond the limitations imposed on them by their Egyptian captors. I believe that there is something very powerful spoken through the passage below in the simple words, "I will bring you up," The Lord planned to lift them up to an entirely new level of freedom, power and purpose.

> *"Go and gather the elders of Israel together, and say to them, 'The Lord God of your fathers, the God of Abraham, of Isaac, and of Jacob, appeared to me, saying, "I have surely visited you and seen what is done to you in Egypt; and I have said I will bring you up out of the affliction of Egypt to the land of the Canaanites and the Hittites and the Amorites and the Perizzites and the Hivites and the Jebusites, to a land flowing with milk and honey."'"*
> (Exodus 3:16-17)

The Lord was announcing through Moses that He was about to establish an entirely new kind of relationship with the people. They needed to begin to prepare to live in this new atmosphere of His presence and His glory. Notice all that the Lord is promising to the people. He promised that His presence, protection, provision, and prosperity were now ready to be released to a nation in slavery. It must have been difficult for them to see this word picture from the depth of their poverty. However, the Lord had already begun the process of bringing them up. It was difficult for Moses to understand how this was possible. He had not yet received the revelation that with God all things are possible. Listen to Moses concerns.

"Then Moses said to the Lord, 'See, You say to me, "'Bring up this people.'" But You have not let me know whom You will send with me. Yet You have said, 'I know you by name, and you have also found grace in My sight.' Now therefore, I pray, if I have found grace in Your sight, show me now Your way, that I may know You and that I may find grace in Your sight. And consider that this nation is Your people.' And He said, 'My Presence will go with you, and I will give you rest.'" (Exodus 33:12-14)

If you were in Moses' shoes, you might be feeling very inadequate at this point. You too would be asking: "How can I possibly accomplish all of this with my limited skills and abilities? How can I persuade people to believe that I am the answer to their prayers? How can I convince them that I am able to accomplish this in their lives? How can I go in to someone like Pharaoh and persuade him to release all of these people? As you ask these questions you can better understand that Moses knew he could not do it alone. He made his concerns known to God and asked for the Lord to be with him through the entire process. Ask yourself: What would the Lord have to show you to convince you that this was your mission and purpose? Then ask: What would you expect of the Lord as you moved forth into your destiny? In a very real sense, this is the Lord's calling on your life right now. He is calling on you to go forth and rescue His people from slavery to sin and death. Who are you to do this? How can you do it without Him? Pray with Moses:

"Then he said to Him, 'If Your Presence does not go with us, do not bring us up from here. For how then will it be known that Your people and I have found grace in Your sight, except You go with us? So we shall be separate, Your people and I, from all the people who are upon the face of the earth.' So the Lord said to Moses, 'I will also do this thing that you have spoken; for you have found grace in My sight, and I know you by name.' And he said, 'Please, show me Your glory.'" (Exodus 33:15-18)

TRANSFERABLE GLORY

We learn something truly amazing about the glory of God in this Mount Sinai manifestation. The glory is transferrable. After spending time in the presence of the Lord, Moses and the people were surprised to discover that the glory of the Lord was on Moses. It was shining on Moses' face, and it frightened the people. I am very visual, and I like to picture these things in my mind. Try to get a mental picture of Moses coming out of the tent of meeting with the glory of God shining on his face. The people probably thought they were seeing a ghost. This is not a normal thing for human beings—or is it? Perhaps this should be the norm for those of us who spend time in the presence of the Lord. After a few hours in the glory, our faces may begin to shine like that of Moses. What do you think? As you prayerfully study the two passages below, see yourself in these accounts, and ask yourself the question: Could this happen to me? Give this question a serious look in your mind and spirit. Is it possible for you?

"Now it was so, when Moses came down from Mount Sinai (and the two tablets of the Testimony were in Moses' hand when he came down from the mountain), that Moses did not know that the skin of his face shone while he talked with Him. So when Aaron and all the children of Israel saw Moses, behold, the skin of his face shone, and they were afraid to come near him." (Exodus 34:29-30)

"And when Moses had finished speaking with them, he put a veil on his face. But whenever Moses went in before the Lord to speak with Him, he would take the veil off until he came out; and he would come out and speak to the children of Israel whatever he had been commanded. And whenever the children of Israel saw the face of Moses, that the skin of Moses' face shone, then Moses would put the veil on his face again, until he went in to speak with Him." (Exodus 34:33-35)

The glory of God was transferred to Moses. It was not something which appeared only once as a sign. It happened every time Moses spent time in the presence of the Lord. I believe that the idea of transferable glory is a challenge to the belief system for most people today. They can accept that it happened to Moses, but have trouble thinking that it might happen for them or others today. This manifestation of the glory on Moses face was not merely a figure of speech. The glow startled and frightened the children of Israel. They could not stay in his presence or listen to him until he covered his face with a veil. Try to picture it in your own mind. I am asking you to co-labor with me in making this experience real in our own lives. This is not merely a story about something that happened a long time ago in a land far away. This is my story and this is your story as well.

It is important to notice that the glory on Moses faded quickly. But the glory which belongs to the Lord will never fade away or be weakened by time. His power, purpose and wisdom will never grow cold or depart from those who are called according to His purpose. If we are going to carry this in our lives, we need to continue to spend time in His presence. We need to establish a place for our own encounters with God. We need to have our own "tent of meeting," and visit there often so that the glory of God can continue to manifest in our lives and ministry.

> *"Therefore, since we have such hope, we use great boldness of speech—unlike Moses, who put a veil over his face so that the children of Israel could not look steadily at the end of what was passing away. But their minds were blinded. For until this day the same veil remains unlifted in the reading of the Old Testament, because the veil is taken away in Christ. But even to this day, when Moses is read, a veil lies on their heart. Nevertheless when one turns to the Lord, the veil is taken away."* (2 Corinthians 3:12-16)

The important thing to grasp right now is that the glory of God can also be transferred to you and me. Have you ever seen the glory of God manifesting on the face of someone who has been in His presence? Has it happened to you? I want to emphasize again that it should be seen on others, and it should be manifest on you after an extended time of intimacy with the Lord. Begin now to believe the Word of God and expect His promises and glory to manifest in you, on you, and through you! Is this a Biblical concept? I believe the answer is "Yes!" as evidenced in the teaching of Paul.

> *"But we all, with unveiled face, beholding as in a mirror the glory of the Lord, are being transformed into the same image from glory to glory, just as by the Spirit of the Lord."* (2 Corinthians 3:18)

REVEALED HIS GLORY IS HIS GOODNESS

When the children of Israel first saw the bread of Heaven, they asked, "What is it?" In fact that is what the Hebrew term manna means. When people first see the glory of God, they often ask the same question: "What is it!" They may become a little frightened when they see the fire, feel the heat, and experience the weighty presence of the Lord. This type of fear is not the reaction the Lord is seeking. He does not want people to recoil and hide from His presence. He has done everything possible to make a way for us to see and experience His glory. He wants you to know that He has a plan, purpose, hope, and destiny for you. He is not showing up to judge, punish, or harm you. When you see the glory, you are seeing something very special about who He is and what He plans for you. You are seeing His goodness, grace, compassion, and mercy in every manifestation of His glory.

"And he said, "Please, show me Your glory." Then He said, "I will make all My goodness pass before you, and I will proclaim the name of the Lord before you. I will be gracious to whom I will be gracious, and I will have compassion on whom I will have compassion." But He said, "You cannot see My face; for no man shall see Me, and live." And the Lord said, "Here is a place by Me, and you shall stand on the rock. So it shall be, while My glory passes by, that I will put you in the cleft of the rock, and will cover you with My hand while I pass by. Then I will take away My hand, and you shall see My back; but My face shall not be seen." (Exodus 33:18-23)

REVEALED MANY OF HIS ATTRIBUTES

Much of what we know about God was given to Moses on Mount Sinai. There the Lord revealed who He is, what He wants, and what He expects. He revealed how He will respond with blessing for those who follow Him, and how He will withhold blessing from those who live in disobedience and rebellion. On the mountain, the Lord revealed many of His awesome attributes to Moses and directed him to teach these things to others. When we do a study of the attributes of God, we should always go back to this profound series of revelations which were demonstrated in His glory on Mount Sinai.

He is holy. Even the ground around Him is holy in His glory presence. Pause and think about what Peter taught, *"But just as he who called you is holy, so be holy in all you do; for it is written: "Be holy, because I am holy."* (1 Peter 1:15-16) This revelation of the Lord as the "Holy One" is not something detached and distant from us. He wants us to understand who He is and then strive to be more and more like Him each day. We need to go from glory to glory into that image! We cannot really do that unless we have the "fear of the Lord" and treat His presence as holy. I experienced this in a profound way during a glory outpouring. After His glory manifested over the church pulpit, I never went back to that place. I moved down to the floor area because the place where He had appeared was too holy and His presence there too heavy for me to stand.

"Then He said, 'Do not draw near this place. Take your sandals off your feet, for the place where you stand is holy ground.' Moreover He said, 'I am the God of your father—the God of Abraham, the God of Isaac, and the God of Jacob.' And Moses hid his face, for he was afraid to look upon God." (Exodus 3:5-6)

He is the One who sees, hears and delivers. The Hebrew people felt abandoned in Egypt during those long years of slavery. They wondered if the Lord was still listening to their prayers. Was He still aware of their circumstances? Did He know what was happening to them and how much they were suffering? They had cried out so many times and only heard silence. They didn't know that the Lord was listening and preparing a great deliverance which had to happen in a certain time with a chosen person. Through Moses, the Lord was making it known that He had not abandoned them. Perhaps you need to hear this as well. Have you been going through some tough times and wondered if the Lord is hearing your prayers? He wants you to know Him as the one who sees, hears, and delivers. He is your God, and has already set in motion all the things needed to bring about your deliverance.

> *"And the Lord said: 'I have surely seen the oppression of My people who are in Egypt, and have heard their cry because of their taskmasters, for I know their sorrows. So I have come down to deliver them out of the hand of the Egyptians, and to bring them up from that land to a good and large land, to a land flowing with milk and honey, to the place of the Canaanites and the Hittites and the Amorites and the Perizzites and the Hivites and the Jebusites. Now therefore, behold, the cry of the children of Israel has come to Me, and I have also seen the oppression with which the Egyptians oppress them.'"*
> (Exodus 3:7-9)

He is the God who created you, knows you, empowers you, and emboldens you. He wants you to know and understand who He is in relationship to you. You must never forget that the One who created you knows everything about you. He has placed in you all the skills, abilities, and gifts you will need to succeed in your destiny. He can speak through you even when you feel inadequate. He can bring healing in your life for those things which have no answer in the field of medicine. He can teach you everything you need to know at the exact moment when you need to know it. He is still your source for wisdom, knowledge, council, understanding and strength. Trust Him! He has you covered!

"So the Lord said to him, 'Who has made man's mouth? Or who makes the mute, the deaf, the seeing, or the blind? Have not I, the Lord? Now therefore, go, and I will be with your mouth and teach you what you shall say.'" (Exodus 4:11-12)

He is a covenant making God who always keeps His part of the agreement. Making covenants is one of God's awesome attributes. He initiates covenants on your behalf and He puts His purpose and power behind the accomplishment of all the good things in your life. He is the God who speaks to you and invites you to receive all the benefits and privileges of those who keep covenant with Him. He always makes covenants which provide far more for you than is required from you. He is the one who has your best interests at heart and covenants to accomplish it for you.

"'Now therefore, if you will indeed obey My voice and keep My covenant, then you shall be a special treasure to Me above all people; for all the earth is Mine. And you shall be to Me a kingdom of priests and a holy nation.' These are the words which you shall speak to the children of Israel." (Exodus 19:5-6)

He desires to be with His people, and teaches them how to be ready for Him. The Lord does not want to be separated far from you. He does not want to hide in the darkness and seem distant to you. He wants to dwell with you and in you. He made this clear when He established His feasts and festivals for His people. He has provided everything you need in order to be consecrated and ready to enter into His presence. At the same time that we celebrate these attributes of the Lord, we must remember that it is still required on our part to honor His presence and respect His holiness. We must still hold to the true and Biblical "fear of the Lord." This too is for our benefit so that we can draw close to Him and experience Him drawing close to us.

"Then the Lord said to Moses, 'Go to the people and consecrate them today and tomorrow, and let them wash their clothes. And let them be ready for the third day. For on the third day the Lord will come down upon Mount Sinai in the sight of all the people. You shall set bounds for the people all around, saying, Take heed to yourselves that you do not go up to the mountain or touch its base. Whoever touches the mountain shall surely be put to death.'" (Exodus 19:10-12)

He is the source of your blessing and favor. He gave a permanent reminder of His faithfulness toward those who follow Him. One of the Lord's first actions on the mountain was to establish a pattern and process for releasing blessing to His people. He is the God who blesses and prevents anyone from bringing a curse on those He has blessed. Notice that receiving the blessing puts the name of the Lord on you. He wants to put His mark—His name—on you as He blesses every aspect of your life and work. He wants to not only give you shalom, but to also establish it for you and your family.

"And the Lord spoke to Moses, saying: 'Speak to Aaron and his sons, saying, This is the way you shall bless the children of Israel. Say to them: The Lord bless you and keep you; The Lord make His face shine upon you, And be gracious to you; The Lord lift up His countenance upon you, And give you peace.' So they shall put My name on the children of Israel, and I will bless them." (Numbers 6:22-27)

In the same way that Moses came to the mountain of the Lord, our journey in the glory begins in this same place. This is not some dusty Old Testament concept without purpose in your life. Listen to the teaching of the writer of Hebrews. He makes it clear that those who have accepted Yeshua ha Messiach have also been allowed to go up the mountain of the Lord. He is no longer untouchable. He is no longer distant and removed from you. He is your God – your "I AM!" He is now calling and inviting you to come up to the mountain top and experience a powerful and life changing manifestation of His glory. Study the two passages below and put yourself into the promises so that you can fully experience this manifestation.

"For you have not come to the mountain that may be touched and that burned with fire, and to blackness and darkness and tempest, and the sound of a trumpet and the voice of words, so that those who heard it begged that the word should not be spoken to them anymore."
(Hebrews 12:18-19)

"But you have come to Mount Zion and to the city of the living God, the heavenly Jerusalem, to an innumerable company of angels, to the general assembly and church of the firstborn who are registered in heaven, to God the Judge of all, to the spirits of just men made perfect, to Jesus the Mediator of the new covenant, and to the blood of sprinkling that speaks better things than that of Abel."
(Hebrews 12:22-24)

God has not changed. He is the same yesterday, today and forever. He is still a consuming fire! He is still to be approached with holy fear and righteousness! He is still to be obeyed and honored. If you want to experience the glory as they did, you must begin to do what they did!

"Therefore, since we are receiving a kingdom which cannot be shaken, let us have grace, by which we may serve God acceptably with reverence and godly fear. For our God is a consuming fire." (Hebrews 12:28-29)

PRAYER

"I have manifested Your name to the men whom You have given Me out of the world. They were Yours, You gave them to Me, and they have kept Your word. Now they have known that all things which You have given Me are from You. For I have given to them the words which You have given Me; and they have received them, and have known surely that I came forth from You; and they have believed that You sent Me. "I pray for them. I do not pray for the world but for those whom You have given Me, for they are Yours. And all Mine are Yours, and Yours are Mine, and I am glorified in them." (John 17:6-10)

SELAH QUESTIONS

1. Describe a mountaintop experience in your own life.

2. What did the Lord reveal about Himself in that experience?

3. How has this experience helped to shape your life and ministry?

4. Ask the Holy Spirit to reveal more to you about this experience and write it down in the space below.

5. How do you plan to press in for more of His glory?

6. In Leviticus chapter nineteen, the Lord says sixteen times, "I Am the Lord." What does "I Am" mean to you?

CHAPTER 3

LEVEL 2: GLORY ON THE PRIESTS

HE PUT HIS GLORY ON THE PRIESTS

"Now He said to Moses, 'Come up to the Lord, you and Aaron, Nadab and Abihu, and seventy of the elders of Israel, and worship from afar. And Moses alone shall come near the Lord, but they shall not come near; nor shall the people go up with him.'" (Exodus 24:1-2)

Notice that Aaron and his sons were not allowed to get as close as Moses to the Lord and His glory. They were called up the mountain, but not allowed to come near the Lord like Moses. Even though they could not get near to the Lord, their call to come up on the mountain was a great honor. This is made very clear when we read that the people were not allowed to come go up the mountain at all. The only exception was the seventy elders invited by the Lord. When Moses drew near and stayed in the presence of the Lord, the glow of God's glory remained on him. However, the priests didn't glow with the glory in the same way as Moses. They were not yet fully ready to carry that level of the glory of God.

In the meantime, the Lord had a different plan for them. The priests had to be dressed up in holy garments in order to reflect the glory of God. It was as if the clothes symbolized what was actualized for Moses. As they put on their holy clothing, they were symbolically putting on the glory of God. The eyes of those who looked at them were not drawn to the men, but to God.

PRIESTS WERE GIVEN HOLY CLOTHING

"Now take Aaron your brother, and his sons with him, from among the children of Israel, that he may minister to Me as priest, Aaron and Aaron's sons: Nadab, Abihu, Eleazar, and Ithamar. And you shall make holy garments for Aaron your brother, for glory and for beauty." (Exodus 28:1-2)

If you consider Aaron's behavior during Moses' first extended stay on the mountain, it is clear that the Lord gives amazing grace to cover sin so that people can still enter His presence and do His will. Think about this and be grateful that no matter what your past may look like, the Lord can restore you and make you fit for service in the Kingdom. The Lord has also made a covering for you so that He does not look on what you have done, but sees what Jesus did for you. He has provided a robe of righteousness for you (Isaiah 61:10). He has taken all of the heaviness off of you and replaced it with a garment of praise (Isaiah 61:3). Notice that He has done all of this so that "He may be glorified" (Isaiah 61:3). He has done all of this for you so that you will know that it is all about Him and His glory.

Notice from the passage above (Exodus 28:2) that the Lord was not just making pretty clothes to impress people. He was telling Moses to make clothes which would first and foremost reflect His glory. The focus is not on the people. The garments are provided so that the priests can minister to the Lord. This may be difficult for you to fully receive as it has been for many others. We have been value programmed in a system which tells us that we are to minister to people and bless the Lord. The opposite was true for the calling of the priests. They were called to minister to the Lord. After this time of ministry they came out of the Temple to bless the people with what they had received during their time in His presence.

SPECIAL GARMENTS FOR THEIR MINISTRY

"And these are the garments which they shall make: a breastplate, an ephod, a robe, a skillfully woven tunic, a turban, and a sash. So they shall make holy garments for Aaron your brother and his sons, that he may minister to Me as priest." (Exodus 28:4)

From this description, we can clearly see that these garments were totally outside the normal style of clothing for the priests and the people. These holy garments were never to be worn outside the specific places and in the manner the Lord commanded. These garments were made to set the priests apart from the people and give them a worthy covering so they could come near the Lord and live. The whole purpose for these garments was to enable them to get closer to the Lord in order to minister to Him. From time to time they had to be reminded of the sacredness of these garments and the limitations on their wear.

"When the priests enter them, they shall not go out of the holy chamber into the outer court; but there they shall leave their garments in which they minister, for they are holy. They shall put on other garments; then they may approach that which is for the people." (Ezekiel 42:14)

In the paragraphs below, we will consider some of the elements of these clothes and what these had to do with ministering to the Lord in the glory. As you consider the relationship between the priestly garments and ministering to the Lord, you must also be aware of the garments the Lord has provided for you. All of us need to understand the nature and necessity of being properly attired when entering the presence of the Lord. Many people have told me that they want intimacy with the Lord on their terms rather than His. This attitude points to a confusion about Who the Lord is and who we are as His servants. You cannot have a relationship of intimacy with the Lord while exhibiting a spirit of disobedience and rebellion.

STONES AS A MEMORIAL FOR SONS

"Then you shall take two onyx stones and engrave on them the names of the sons of Israel: six of their names on one stone and six names on the other stone, in order of their birth. With the work of an engraver in stone, like the engravings of a signet, you shall engrave the two stones with the names of the sons of Israel. You shall set them in settings of gold. And you shall put the two stones on the shoulders of the ephod as memorial stones for the sons of Israel. So Aaron shall bear their names before the Lord on his two shoulders as a memorial." (Exodus 28:9-12)

The priests could clearly see that their service was not just for themselves. The two stones on the shoulders reminded the priests that in all of their service, they were doing it on behalf of all the tribes and all the people. Aaron was directed to "bear their names" on his shoulders when he ministered to the Lord. The word "bear" is very significant. They were to "bear" (or carry) the weight of the people's sin and atone for it before the Lord. They were to "bear" the praises of the people and minister them to the Lord.

The Lord has said that we are to be a kingdom of priests and kings. As priests, we too are to shoulder the burdens of our people. We are to bear their names in prayer before the Lord. The dress code is different, but the responsibilities are still the same. As we lift up intercessory prayers to the Lord, we "bear their names" as did the priests of old. Are you ready to shoulder these responsibilities? If you want to host the glory, you must be faithful and obedient to the calling and commands of the Lord. Remember that the Lord is still looking for intercessors (Isaiah 59:16). He is still looking for those who are willing to build a wall and stand in the gap (Ezekiel 22:30).

BREASTPLATE OF JUDGEMENT

"You shall make the breastplate of judgment. Artistically woven according to the workmanship of the ephod you shall make it: of gold, blue, purple, and scarlet thread, and fine woven linen, you shall make it. It shall be doubled into a square: a span shall be its length, and a span shall be its width. And you shall put settings of stones in it, four rows of stones:" (Exodus 28:15-17a)

I want to call your attention once more to how specific and descriptive the Lord is about all of the things He told Moses to prepare. The specificity makes it clear that these things are very important to the Lord. This should encourage us to value them as well. In our case, the focus is not so much on the physical garments but the spiritual covering we need in order to experience His glory and learn to be better hosts of His presence. In Ephesians 6:14, Paul tells us to wear a breastplate of righteousness; *"Stand therefore, having girded your waist with truth, having put on the breastplate of righteousness,"* Is there some kind of connection between judgment and righteousness?

Let's take a closer look at the "breastplate of judgment." The term "judgment" is used here to make a special point about the purpose of both the breastplate and its contents. When most Christians see the term judgment, they think about a time of judgment like that which is to come at the end of the age. They think first of courtrooms, thrones, and judges. The term was used in a different manner in the Old Testament. The primary function of judging was to determine the will of God for the persons involved. In other words, judging how He desires for them to live and how to understand the destiny He has established for them. Are they currently in that close relationship with Him which derives from following the path He has set before them? The final step in judgment is to determine what they need to do in order to get back into a right relationship with Him.

And the stones shall have the names of the sons of Israel, twelve according to their names, like the engravings of a signet, each one with its own name; they shall be according to the twelve tribes." (Exodus 28:21)

The outer portion of the breastplate of judgment was covered with twelve stones set in four rows. These stones were each representative of one of the twelve tribes of Israel and the name of each tribe was inscribed on one of the stones. These stones pointed to the area of responsibility for handling the judgments of the Lord. The priests did not serve only their own tribe, but all the tribes of Israel when making judgments. It is interesting that by putting the breastplate over the chest of the priest, the Lord makes it clear that this is a matter of the heart. Like Yeshua who was to come later, they were to love, bless, and atone for the sins of all the family of God. In the same way, when we are obedient to Yeshua, we are concerned for the entire world and lift up prayers of intercession for the salvation of souls around the world.

"So Aaron shall bear the names of the sons of Israel on the breastplate of judgment over his heart, when he goes into the holy place, as a memorial before the Lord continually. And you shall put in the breastplate of judgment the Urim and the Thummim, and they shall be over Aaron's heart when he goes in before the Lord. So Aaron shall bear the judgment of the children of Israel over his heart before the Lord continually." (Exodus 28:29-30)

It is an awesome and holy responsibility to carry a memorial for all people before the Lord. The priests had to be prayerfully and carefully prepared to go before the Lord. Shouldn't we do the same? This is made even more clear in the fact that the "Urim and the Thummin" were carried inside the breastplate of judgment. We don't know exactly what they were like, but the scriptures make it clear that the Lord gave judgments, instructions, and commands through their use. When the King asked if they were to go to war, the answer often came through the "Urim and Thummin." When a decision had to be made between two people with opposing views, these items were used to determine the will of God. All kinds of decisions were made through the use of these items, and the Lord's people were certain that the will of the God was revealed in their use.

The detailed instructions for the breastplate of judgment, remind us that we need to put more focus on the preparation of our hearts before we enter into His presence. Remember who is allowed to ascend the hill of the Lord (Psalm 24:4, *"He who has clean hands and a pure heart,"*). We must get our hearts cleansed and filled with divine love before moving close to Him. These instructions and principles were not given to merely last for a short period of time or for a limited number of people. This is for all generations and for all the people of the Lord. We are to hand them down from one generation to the next just as the Lord instructed.

"That son who becomes priest in his place shall put them on for seven days, when he enters the tabernacle of meeting to minister in the holy place." (Exodus 29:30)

We are never left without the resources needed to accomplish all of these great things for the Lord. The Lord has given very specific instructions in His Word. The Lord has given us Yeshua ha Messiach as our intercessor and mediator. He has given us an invitation to come into the "Secret Place," and He has provided all we need for a covering in His presence. Perhaps this is a good time for you to lift these things up to the Lord in prayer. I offer to you as a guide the prayer of David given in Psalm 132. It was used by those ascending Mount Zion in preparation for entering His presence.

"Let us go into His tabernacle; Let us worship at His footstool. Arise, O Lord, to Your resting place, You and the ark of Your strength. Let Your priests be clothed with righteousness, And let Your saints shout for joy." (Psalm 132:7-9)

DIADEM: HOLINESS TO THE LORD

"You shall also make a plate of pure gold and engrave on it, like the engraving of a signet: HOLINESS TO THE Lord. And you shall put it on a blue cord, that it may be on the turban; it shall be on the front of the turban. So it shall be on Aaron's forehead, that Aaron may bear the iniquity of the holy things which the children of Israel hallow in all their holy gifts; and it shall always be on his forehead, that they may be accepted before the Lord." (Exodus 28:36-38)

Many people have a mistaken idea about what holiness means. For these people, the meaning of this word is limited to personal piety or individual perfection. However, we must remember that Biblical holiness is about being separated for a purpose. It means that we have been separated to God and for His purposes. The Diadem proclaimed to all (especially to the one wearing it) that they had been separated from the things of the world and of the flesh to be totally dedicated and consecrated to the service of the Lord. The priest entering the Lord's presence was giving his personal testimony of commitment through the wearing of the Diadem.

Perhaps, we should live and serve as if this Diadem was attached over our foreheads. Have you separated yourself from the things of the flesh in order to serve the Lord wholeheartedly? This is a good time to commit or recommit your life and service to Him. Remember that without holiness no one will see the Lord (Hebrews 12:14). Do you desire to live in intimacy with the Lord? Then you must live in holiness unto Him. It is the way He has established for us. It is the only way available to us. The Diadem is a powerful reminder of who we are and Whose we are!

The diadem had a magnificent and holy purpose. It allowed Aaron and any other priest wearing it to *"bear the iniquity of the holy things,"* along with all the offerings of the people which they brought to Him. Being holy not only opens the door for us to see Him, but also provides a covering for all we do and all we give to Him. It is the way of holiness which we desire to follow. Remember Isaiah 35:8, *"A highway shall be there, and a road, and it shall be called the Highway of Holiness. The unclean shall not pass over it, But it shall be for others. Whoever walks the road, although a fool, shall not go astray."* If we desire to walk with Him and follow His ways, this is the pathway for us to follow.

SPECIAL FOOD TO MAKE THEM HOLY

"Then Aaron and his sons shall eat the flesh of the ram, and the bread that is in the basket, by the door of the tabernacle of meeting." (Exodus 29:32)

People today are extremely health conscious. Many constantly talk about every item of food and drink and judge whether it should or should not be consumed. Some people today are like "food police," who not only judge their own behavior but try to enforce it on others. Even if we don't truly appreciate their actions, they may be on to something good. The Lord made it clear that food can be one of the ways in which He transmits holiness to His people. In the days of the Temple there were people designated to serve as "food police." They had real power and the authority to enforce the rules. They discerned between the clean and unclean; the holy and the profane. Your continued welcome into the place of the Lord was determined by your personal spiritual cleanliness.

The interesting thing in this teaching is that while the priests are to prevent the unclean or unholy from eating the food, it was the food which was making them holy. Each time they ate the food they experienced a kind of elevation in their ability to minister to Him. The Lord gave very specific instructions which were often expanded on or changed by the religious leaders. Instead of being a source of blessing, these altered rules and regulations often became a burden too great to carry.

Is there an equivalent for us today? As a kingdom of priests, we too have access through the Holy Spirit to the Bread of Heaven, and those who eat it are elevated to higher levels of service to the Lord. The Temple in Jerusalem is gone, and now the temple of the Lord is in us. He feeds us with spiritual food to nourish us in spirit, soul, and body. The Lord is good all the time and His mercy endures forever.

"This is the consecrated portion for Aaron and his sons, from the offerings made by fire to the Lord, on the day when Moses presented them to minister to the Lord as priests. The Lord commanded this to be given to them by the children of Israel, on the day that He anointed them, by a statute forever throughout their generations." (Leviticus 7:35-36)

Providing food for the priests was a statute which the Lord commanded to be followed throughout all generations. Does this mean that it is still in effect? I believe the answer is both yes and no. It is still a statute to be followed, but not in the old way. Without a Temple, those types of food are no longer available. So the Lord has provided something different which is actually more holy. Meditate on the full meaning of John 6:35, *"And Jesus said to them, "I am the bread of life. He who comes to Me shall never hunger, and he who believes in Me shall never thirst."* May we always acknowledge His gifts and lift up our praise and thanks to Him for providing all we need to feed our spirits and souls. I like to use the words of Psalm 103 to express my gratitude. This is a good time to make this your prayer!

"Bless the Lord, O my soul; And all that is within me, bless His holy name! Bless the Lord, O my soul, and forget not all His benefits: Who forgives all your iniquities, Who heals all your diseases, Who redeems your life from destruction, Who crowns you with lovingkindness and tender mercies, Who satisfies your mouth with good things, so that your youth is renewed like the eagle's." (Psalm 103:1-5)

From the beginning of the Lord's relationship with Abraham and all His decedents, He established a plan of blessing and favor. This pattern is continued through the service of the priesthood. As such, it is also a pattern for you and me. We are blessed so that we can be a blessing. The more we bless the Lord and all His people the more He blesses us. When the Lord blessed the priests through the holy food, He enabled and charged them to carry His blessing to His people.

"Then the priests, the Levites, arose and blessed the people, and their voice was heard; and their prayer came up to His holy dwelling place, to heaven." (2 Chronicles 30:27)

LIMITATIONS TO APPROACHING THE GLORY

"Now when these things had been thus prepared, the priests always went into the first part of the tabernacle, performing the services. But into the second part the high

65

priest went alone once a year, not without blood, which he offered for himself and for the people's sins committed in ignorance; the Holy Spirit indicating this, that the way into the Holiest of All was not yet made manifest while the first tabernacle was still standing." (Hebrews 9:6-8)

Many people do not do well with limitations. During my days as an active duty army chaplain I was stationed for several years at Fort Dix, New Jersey. It was during this time that the casinos in Atlantic City were opened. On a day off, I went with two other chaplains to investigate and see what the casinos were like. When we arrived, we were faced with a sign which said, "No coat and tie – no admittance!" I shrugged my shoulders and started to walk away with one of the other chaplains. Then we heard a scuffling sound coming from the door of the casino. As we turned to see what all the commotion was about, we were surprised to see our friend being thrown out by the bouncers. As he emerged from the door, he dusted himself off and said, "That has been my problem all of my life. I never thought those signs were for me."

Many people have this same attitude about life and the estab-lished rules of society. They believe that they are the exception to all of the rules. They go through life with the belief that the rules were made for other people and not for them. Perhaps you know someone like this. Or, maybe you see things this way too. It is difficult for most people to abide by all the rules, but it is especially challenging for these people. For this reason, the Lord had to warn the people over and over about the boundaries around Him and His glory. The people who were allowed to go up the mountain waited for permission from the Lord. In the same way, those allowed into the Tabernacle were limited to the Priests and some of the Levites when it was being packed up to move or when it was being set up after they came to a resting place. Other than these exceptions, only Moses and those mentioned in the passage above from the book of Hebrews were allowed to enter.

Notice that the number of those who could enter grew smaller as they got closer to the place of His presence. The people camped around the Tabernacle, but at a distance. The Levites camped closest to the Tabernacle and the tent of meeting. Only the priests could enter the "holy place," and only the high priest could enter the "most holy place." Even the high priest had limitations. He could only enter once a year on the Day of Atonement. These rules and limitations had to be repeated often to ensure the protection of the people. I have heard many people say they storm heaven with their intercessory prayers. How does this kind of theology line up with the limitations the Lord has placed on those coming into His presence? Are any of the rules appropriate for today? I believe that the rules still apply and the wise among us respect and honor the presence of the Lord. This is an important part of manifesting "the fear of the Lord." People who ignore the Word of God will have difficulty establishing and maintaining intimacy with Him.

ONLY AT THE INVITIATION OF THE LORD

"Now the Lord spoke to Moses after the death of the two sons of Aaron, when they offered profane fire before the Lord, and died; and the Lord said to Moses: 'Tell Aaron your brother not to come at just any time into the Holy Place inside the veil, before the mercy seat which is on the ark, lest he die; for I will appear in the cloud above the mercy seat.'" (Leviticus 16:1-2)

We like for things to be done at our convenience and on our time schedule. I believe this is why the fast food industry has flourished so much throughout the world. We want things when we want them, and we don't like to wait. We struggle with the notion that we are "not to come at just any time into the Holy Place." There is an attitude prevalent in many parts of the church which views the Lord as the one who is required to meet our needs whenever we come to Him and ask.

During my time in the seminary, I had to work in order to cover my expenses. One of my jobs was in the seminary print shop. Someone had clipped and stapled a cartoon on the wall which expressed one of their frustrations in serving customers. In the cartoon, a man was standing at the counter talking with the clerk. He said, "Of course I want it today. If I had wanted it tomorrow, I would have brought it in tomorrow!" Many people relate more closely with the customer than the clerk in this cartoon.

This raises a question for me. Do we still need to follow these rules today? I think the answer is both "yes and no." "Yes," we need to honor and respect the Lord and enter His presence at appropriate times. And "No!" because the Lord has made the Holy Spirit available to us at all times, we can lift up our praises and petitions at any time trusting that the Holy Spirit will make it all appropriate for the Lord. We can count on the Lord dwelling within us just as the Lord promised (John 14:23). He is always close at hand, because He abides in us. On the other hand, when we desire to enter the "Secret Place" of the "Most High," we do that by invitation only. Perhaps this is why many have not experienced being carried by the Spirit into His presence. We need to learn the protocol of heaven and honor the procedures of the Kingdom if we want to walk and talk with the Lord.

ONLY WHEN PROPERLY COVERED

"Thus Aaron shall come into the Holy Place: with the blood of a young bull as a sin offering, and of a ram as a burnt offering. He shall put the holy linen tunic and the linen trousers on his body; he shall be girded with a linen sash, and with the linen turban he shall be attired. These are holy garments. Therefore he shall wash his body in water, and put them on. And he shall take from the congregation of the children of Israel two kids of the goats as a sin offering, and one ram as a burnt offering." (Leviticus 16:3-5)

Most of the old dress codes have been scrapped in the last few years. We live in a world which has embraced the casual over the formal. When I visited a friend in Hawaii, he invited me to go to dinner and said that the dress code was "island formal." I asked what that meant and he told me that it meant sandals, shorts, and a tank top. Even in much of the business world, the three piece suit has been replaced by slacks and an open collared shirt. Many churches have a very casual dress code today. It seems as if anything goes in some of these services. However, most churches have to stop from time to time and establish some rules because people tend to take everything too far.

Is there a dress code today for entering the Lord's presence and hosting the glory? What do you think? The Lord was so specific in establishing the dress code for the Tabernacle and the Temple. This leads me to believe that this is important to Him. This does not mean that we all have to go out and purchase a "high priest suit." In fact, I am not comfortable with the idea of dressing in the way the Lord specified so clearly for a limited number of people. I want to be obedient to Him because this is the standard set for us by Yeshua ha Messiach. Every passage about abiding in Him or dwelling with Him begins with the phrase "if you obey." Obedience is still the key today.

So, what is the dress code for today? I mentioned this in the beginning of this chapter, but it is good to consider it again. First, we must come before Him wearing the "robe of righteousness." You can't go out and purchase this robe. It is a gift from the Lord (Isaiah 61:10). In addition to this robe, we need to be attired in a "garment of praise." Again, you can't go out and purchase one. This too is a gift from the Lord (Isaiah 61:3). There is one more covering that we need in order to come into His presence. We must always be covered with a cloak of humility. Don't worry about this one either. The Lord has provided everything we need.

"Therefore, brothers, since we have confidence to enter the Most Holy Place by the blood of Jesus, by a new and

living way opened for us through the curtain, that is, his body, and since we have a great priest over the house of God, let us draw near to God with a sincere heart in full assurance of faith, having our hearts sprinkled to cleanse us from a guilty conscience and having our bodies washed with pure water." (Hebrews 10:19-22, NIV)

PROTECTED BY A SMOKE SCREEN

"Then he shall take a censer full of burning coals of fire from the altar before the Lord, with his hands full of sweet incense beaten fine, and bring it inside the veil. And he shall put the incense on the fire before the Lord, that the cloud of incense may cover the mercy seat that is on the Testimony, lest he die." (Leviticus 16:12-13)

In this second level of the manifestation of His glory, the priests were given a limited opportunity to actually see Him and they were protected by a physical cloud of smoke which covered over their flesh and the sins of the flesh. At this point they had not been given permission to see Him face to face. Even Moses was not allowed to see His face. When the Lord let Moses see His glory, it was only revealed from the back. This was because they had not received the covering of the Lord which was to come through the completed work of Jesus Christ on the cross. They were not to look on Him. And He chose not to look on them at this point, because their sin had not yet been covered.

Things are very different for us, because of what Christ did for us. We don't need a smoke screen or a veil. The Lord ripped the veil open from top to bottom, so that we could have access to Him with the blood of Jesus. The Temple, like the veil, has been removed so that we have full access. Now, He dwells in the temple which is in our hearts. The Lord has done this and it is awesome! When He looks at us, He sees the covering provided by Jesus. He also smells the fragrance of Christ on us. *"For we are to God the fragrance of Christ among those who are being saved and among those who are perishing."* (2 Corinthians 2:15)

ALWAYS WITH THE BLOOD

"He shall take some of the blood of the bull and sprinkle it with his finger on the mercy seat on the east side; and before the mercy seat he shall sprinkle some of the blood with his finger seven times. 'Then he shall kill the goat of the sin offering, which is for the people, bring its blood inside the veil, do with that blood as he did with the blood of the bull, and sprinkle it on the mercy seat and before the mercy seat."' (Leviticus 16:14-15)

In the words of the old Hymn by George A. Young, "*God leads us along*" (Public domain): "*Some through the waters, some through the flood, some through the fire, but all through the blood;*" The priests of old came into His presence with the blood of animals, but we come with a far better covering. We come into His presence covered by the blood of the Lamb. We have been sprinkled and covered by the blood of Jesus and we must have this covering if we are to safely come into His presence. Take note; this covering is necessary for those who desire to experience His glory and the power of His presence.

IMMEDIATELY DISCIPLINED FOR DISOBEDIENCE

"Also let the priests who come near the Lord consecrate themselves, lest the Lord break out against them." (Exodus 19:22)

In order to keep the way open into His presence, the Lord immediately dealt with any and all disobedience. This was not about arbitrary rules or His anger and desire to punish. It was about His grace and His desire to dwell with His people. If

71

anything happened to produce separation, it was dealt with immediately. We see this so clearly in the restoration of Aaron the priest after he made the golden calf idol. The Lord made immediate corrections so that Aaron could be restored to his calling as the Priest of the Lord.

Now there was one outstanding exception to this rule. "*And Nadab and Abihu died when they offered profane fire before the Lord.*" (Numbers 26:61) Remember that the Lord warned them in advance about the penalty for disobedience. Their behavior was so brazen and it set an extremely bad example for the people. Yet, we may wonder why this happened to them as opposed to other actions by some of the people. As I mentioned above, this concerned me as well. So, I investigated the scriptures concerning this event very carefully, and I believe that it is clear what the problem was in these two sons of Aaron. It is so important that I want to go through it again with you in a little more detail. Too many people want to be members of the "anything goes church."

> "*Then Nadab and Abihu, the sons of Aaron, each took his censer and put fire in it, put incense on it, and offered profane fire before the Lord, which He had not commanded them. So fire went out from the Lord and devoured them, and they died before the Lord. And Moses said to Aaron, "This is what the Lord spoke, saying: 'By those who come near Me I must be regarded as holy; And before all the people I must be glorified.'" So Aaron held his peace.*" (Leviticus 10:1-3)

Think about this as we ask again, "What was really behind the behavior of Nadab and Abihu which caused this response from the Lord?" I believe that there were at least two things in this event which necessitated this response from the Lord. Both of these things revealed a total lack of respect or fear of the Lord. The first factor is clearly pointed out in the passage above.

They offered "profane fire before the Lord." What does the word "profane" mean here? They jumped in without permission and offered the kind of fire that pagans used to worship idols. They blatantly disobeyed the specific instructions of the Lord which had just been given to them. They treated the Lord the same way idols are treated. This was not acceptable then and it is not acceptable now. There is a difference between the profane and the holy; the clean and the unclean. We are to teach it and model it in all our service to the Lord.

The second problem with the behavior of Nadab and Abihu is not as clearly stated. To understand it, you have to read the passages which immediately follow this account. The Lord spoke to Aaron and gave him another rule about entering into the Lord's presence. Do not come before the Lord if you are drunk or under the influence of drugs which limit your ability to appropriately respond to the Lord. Study Leviticus 10:8-11 once again and think about the meaning of this passage of scripture for you, and for your service to the Lord.

Obviously from this immediate correction from the Lord, Aaron's two sons had been intoxicated and acted in a very inappropriate way under the influence of alcohol. It is true that the Lord is very gracious and His mercy endures forever. On the other hand, we are repeatedly told that obedience is the key to hosting the glory of God. We need to feel the love and grace of God, but we also need to understand the "fear of the Lord" and always show Him the respect, honor, praise, worship and glory He deserves. He is not a man. He is the Holy God who created and maintains the entire Universe, and we are to interact with Him accordingly.

"Now this is the main point of the things we are saying: We have such a High Priest, who is seated at the right hand of the throne of the Majesty in the heavens, a Minister of the sanctuary and of the true tabernacle which the Lord erected, and not man." (Hebrews 8:1-2)

PRAYER

"Now I am no longer in the world, but these are in the world, and I come to You. Holy Father, keep through Your name those whom You have given Me, that they may be one as We are. While I was with them in the world, I kept them in Your name. Those whom You gave Me I have kept; and none of them is lost except the son of perdition, that the Scripture might be fulfilled. But now I come to You, and these things I speak in the world, that they may have My joy fulfilled in themselves. I have given them Your word; and the world has hated them because they are not of the world, just as I am not of the world. I do not pray that You should take them out of the world, but that You should keep them from the evil one." (John 17:11-15)

SELAH QUESTIONS

1. Write a short explanation of what Exodus 19:6 means to you, *"And you shall be to Me a kingdom of priests and a holy nation.' These are the words which you shall speak to the children of Israel."*

2. Does this apply to you and the church today? If so, in what way?

3. How are we to dress in order to enter into His presence?

4. What must we do in order to better host the Glory?

5. In what ways have you experienced the Glory of God in the temple of your heart?

CHAPTER 4

LEVEL 3: GLORY IN THE TABERNACLE

—~∾∾~—

D o you like power statements? I really like the power statements of the Lord given to us in His Word. In the natural, most power statements are very brief and often appear as simple phrases pointing to a great idea or important truth. On the other hand, the power statements of God come in all sizes to meet all needs. One of these power statements of the Lord is found in the twenty ninth chapter of the book of Exodus. Read it aloud! Why is it important to read scriptures aloud? The answer is in Romans 10:17, *"So then faith comes by hearing, and hearing by the word of God."* Read this passage from Exodus slowly, piece by piece, so that you may absorb more of its meaning into your spirit.

> *"This shall be a continual burnt offering throughout your generations at the door of the tabernacle of meeting before the Lord, where I will meet you to speak with you. And there I will meet with the children of Israel, and the tabernacle shall be sanctified by My glory. So I will consecrate the tabernacle of meeting and the altar. I will also consecrate both Aaron and his sons to minister to Me as priests. I will dwell among the children of Israel*

and will be their God. And they shall know that I am the Lord their God, who brought them up out of the land of Egypt, that I may dwell among them. I am the Lord their God." (Exodus 29:42-46)

Several things made a powerful impression on me as I studied this passage. The first was located in the middle of the passage: "*and the tabernacle shall be sanctified by My glory.*" The tabernacle was cleansed and consecrated, but only the presence of God's glory could actually sanctify it, and this is exactly what He wanted to do. As you think about these passages of scripture, try to see them in relation to your own life and spiritual journey. As you study the Word in this way, ask yourself, "What does this say about the temple of God in me?" Is the Lord sanctifying the temple in you by the presence of His glory? If not, what do you need to do to allow Him to bring this about in your spirit?

Next, I focused on the statement, "*I will dwell among the children of Israel and will be their God.*" This is such an awesome thought, and it is exactly what Jesus was talking about in John 14:23. Something really powerful had to happen in order for Him to dwell with Israel. It was accomplished through the building of the Tabernacle and the establishment of the entire sacrificial system. Again, remember that the actual word in the Torah which was translated as the English word "sacrifice" is "*karban*" ("*korban*" in the Greek) and it's true meaning is actually better defined as "to draw close" to God. This has always been God's desire for you and for me. He wants to be close to us and He has done everything necessary to make that possible. All He needs to accomplish it now is our willingness. Are you ready to draw near to Him and to let Him draw near to you (James 4:8)?

A third power statement in this passage which really spoke to me was in the final verse: "*I am the Lord their God.*" I love all of the "I AM" statements in the Bible and I try to highlight each one every time I read it. He makes this statement hundreds of times in the Bible. He sincerely wants us to understand and embrace the idea that He is our Lord. We belong to Him and He is our God! Amen? Meditate on this and then look at Psalm 100:3, *"Know that the Lord, He is God; It is He who has made us, and not we ourselves; we are His people and the sheep of His pasture."* There is power in this verse, and it is released when you read it aloud over and over. Let it build up in your spirit and become the power and authority behind your testimony!

GOD WAS VERY SPECIFIC ABOUT HOW THE TABERNACLE WAS TO BE BUILT

"According to all that I show you, that is, the pattern of the tabernacle and the pattern of all its furnishings, just so you shall make it." (Exodus 25:9)

During Moses' extended visits with the Lord on Mount Sinai, he was taught all the details necessary to build the Tabernacle. In the Bible, we have an extensive account about this detailed description which the Lord gave for the structure and for all of its furnishings. In addition, the Lord somehow showed it to Moses. It seems clear that the Lord used a series of detailed visions to reveal all of the details to Moses. I have often tried to picture this in my mind, because it is such a beautiful account of how the Lord can reveal something in so much detail, in order to make it prophetically significant for all the future generations of the Lord's people. In the passage above, the Lord tells Moses to build it just like he saw it on the mountain.

It is obvious from Moses detailed account of the Tabernacle and its furnishings that he sensed the extreme importance this had for the Lord and the children of Israel. Can you sense how important it is to the Lord to find a way to tabernacle with His people? This inspires me to desire it with all of my heart. I want Him to tabernacle with me and I want to spend as much time with Him as possible. How about you? Begin now to see yourself in this story and seek revelation knowledge about how you can establish a place in your own home where you can meet with God face to face. In Moses day, only one man was allowed to do this. However, in our day, the Lord has made it possible for every born-again, Spirit filled, and Spirit led believer to have this kind of relationship with Him.

BUILDING A HOLY HABITATION

This kind of project cannot be accomplished by guess work. In the same way, if the Lord is going to tabernacle with you, it will be in accordance with His will and His plan. Let this be both an example and an inspiration for you to establish such a place for the Lord to dwell with you. As you study how God instructed them in detail about how they were to make it a holy habitation, seek the wisdom of the Lord in building your own sukkah (booth). I also refer you to Chapter 6 of my book, "Gatekeepers Arise!" This entire chapter details how you can guard your heart to keep it a holy habitation for His glory.

You can find the details of the Tabernacle in the book of Exodus Chapters 25-30. Many people simply glance over or skip this part of the Bible altogether because they don't really see the significance of it. If you truly desire to host the glory, go back to this section of the Bible and read it with the inspiration of the Holy Spirit. Jesus promised that the Holy Spirit would guide you into all truth (John 16:13). Place a specific claim on this promise, and seek His counsel for what you should receive from this detailed description of every part of His Holy Habitation.

GLORY DESCENDS FROM THE MOUNTAIN

Up to this point in the account, the Glory was still positioned on the mountain. The revelations released by the Lord then flowed down through Moses and various others who were allowed to go up into His presence. At this point in their history, something new begins to happen for the children of Israel. Rather than having more and more people go up the mountain, the glory of God comes down into the camp where the people live. All of the other manifestations of the glory had to happen first so that a holy habitation could be prepared to welcome His powerful and holy presence. Now that the priests had been commissioned and consecrated to minister to the Lord, the hour had come for the Lord to take up residence in His new abode.

"In the tabernacle of meeting, outside the veil which is before the Testimony, Aaron and his sons shall tend it from evening until morning before the Lord. It shall be a statute forever to their generations on behalf of the children of Israel." (Exodus 27:21)

The sacrificial system had been established by the Lord so that He could come near to His people and they could draw near to Him. Now, they were seeing it happen just as the Lord promised. This was all a magnificent move of God in order to draw them (and us) into His presence. He did all of this to provide a covering of glory over human sin so that people could be close to Him. This is similar to the glory covering which has been missing since Adam and Eve lost it in the Garden.

With the provision of this covering, the Lord made His people holy (set apart for Him and His purposes) so they could come near to Him. This was very good news for them as it is for us. However, the people did not respond whole heartedly. They drew close one day and moved away another day. The sacrificial system provided them a way to cleanse their rebellion and sin so that they could come back and be restored into a right relationship with Him. This response to the Lord is still prevalent today. People still draw close and then fall away. People still need a way to receive reconciliation and restoration.

At this point we see a difference between the way it was made available to the people in ancient times and the way the

Lord makes it available to us. We no longer have a system of sacrifices which cleanse our hands and hearts so that we can once again approach the Lord. However, this does not mean that all is lost. The Lord took care of everything in the one pure and perfect sacrifice of Jesus. Now, all we need to do is sincerely and wholeheartedly repent and ask the Lord to forgive and restore us so that we can walk again in intimacy with Him. He is faithful and good, and He will accomplish it for those who humbly and sincerely seek Him. I am reminded again of that ancient way of expressing praise: "The Lord is good! His mercy endures forever!" Say it aloud several times with increasing intensity. It still works today. It invokes His presence, and the glory still comes down to His people. As I speak it over and over I feel the presence of the Lord come over me and enter into my heart! As I continue to make this affirmation of praise the presence of His glory gets stronger and heavier. Amen!

HIS GLORY WAS VISIBLE

This is something I get excited about, and I hope that you share the joy and expectancy of the appearing of the Lord. In the days of Moses, His glory was visible to everyone in the cloud by day and the column of fire by night. I pray for this to manifest again as we draw near to Him so that the unsaved may see it and experience an ever increasing desire to draw near to Him. I pray that the Lord will come in power again to set us apart and clear away every spot of doubt and rebellion. I pray that the cloud of His glory will once again be seen among His people! Several truly awesome things happened when the glory of the Lord appeared in the cloud and in the fire. Look closely and think deeply about each of these promises of the Lord as we examine them in more detail.

HIS GLORY SANCTIFIED THEM

Look again at Exodus 19:43-46 as we go deeper into our study of the glory. The word "sanctified" in verse forty three is from the Hebrew root word "qadash" which can also be translated as "holy" or "set apart." The adjective to describe those set apart in this way is "qadosh." In this case, The Lord set the tabernacle apart for His dwelling. You could also say that His glory made it holy. This was awesome, but His work of sanctification did not end with the physical tent and its furnishings. The presence of His glory also made Aaron, his sons, and others who followed in the priestly office holy. From many Biblical accounts we know that they did not become perfect in the human sense of the word. They were set apart and declared holy in the presence of His glory.

Do you think this is still possible today? Can we still get into His glory and be set apart for His purposes? Can we be called holy when this happens? This is obviously the Lord's intent, because we see in this passage that he also set the people apart and they too became holy by His decree and by His presence. The Lord made his intentions for all of us very clear in this passage. He wants to dwell in our midst and He will do everything necessary to make that possible. All we have to do is receive it and live in accordance with His plan.

It is important to notice that the Lord made His intentions abundantly clear in this passage of scripture. In verse 29:43, we are told that He did all of this so that He could meet with His people. In verse 29:45, He goes further to make it clear that His plan is not just to visit briefly with His people, but to dwell with them and to be their God. Finally in verse 29:46, the Lord said that all of this was so that they would know that He was their God. To anchor the thought, He said it again: "I AM the Lord their God." This was not just for that group at that time. This is still the Lord's plan and purpose as His glory comes to dwell with you and me. Amen?

GLORY COVERED THE TABERNACLE

"Then the cloud covered the tabernacle of meeting, and the glory of the Lord filled the tabernacle. And Moses was not able to enter the tabernacle of meeting, because the cloud rested above it, and the glory of the Lord filled the tabernacle." (Exodus 40:34-35)

It may be difficult for many people to fully understand this passage if they have not experienced His weighty presence as described in the passage above. I have personally experienced this kind of presence when the weight fell and I was unable to move under it. I have also seen it happen to many other people. When this falls on you, you cannot even move your fingers. You certainly cannot minister, preach or teach in the presence of His glory. These experiences have helped me to more fully understand and appreciate the meaning of passages like the one above.

In the presence of His glory, the Lord does the ministry. Even Moses could not enter the Tabernacle when the Glory was there. The same thing happened when the Glory manifested during the dedication of the Temple in the days of Solomon. The priests could not minister. When the Lord fills the house, there is no room for anyone or anything else. When this happens, we know with certainty that all of the glory belongs to Him. We cannot claim any of it, because we know that it is His work alone. We are simply not capable of doing the things which happen in the glory. It is the Lord and it is Him only.

HE TOOK COMMAND OF HIS ARMIES

"Now the Lord spoke to Moses in the Wilderness of Sinai, in the tabernacle of meeting, on the first day of the second month, in the second year after they had come out of the land of Egypt, saying: Take a census of all the

*congregation of the children of Israel, by their families,
by their fathers' houses, according to the number of
names, every male individually, from twenty years old
and above—all who are able to go to war in Israel. You
and Aaron shall number them by their armies.*" (Numbers 1:1-3)

When the Lord sent His glory to dwell among them, He continued to reveal more and more of Himself and His plan for His people. It may have been a surprise for them to learn that they were His "armies" and He was their Commander in Chief. When they escaped from slavery in Egypt, Moses gave the Lord a new title: "*The Lord is a man of war; The Lord is His name. Pharaoh's chariots and his army He has cast into the sea; His chosen captains also are drowned in the Red Sea.*" (Exodus 15:3-4) When they entered the "Promised Land" by way of war, they were very glad that this relationship had been established. This understanding of their relationship with the Lord continued through the time of Isaiah 42:13, "*The Lord shall go forth like a mighty man; He shall stir up His zeal like a man of war. He shall cry out, yes, shout aloud; He shall prevail against His enemies.*" Do you and I still understand this today? I pray that the Lord will reveal His truth to you!

As soon as they emerged from Egypt, the Lord began to prepare them for war. He personally protected them from enemies until they were battle-ready and could move forward without fear. Before they experienced war, they needed to see the awesome power the Lord could bring to bear against any enemy force. Then they needed to learn to immediately obey His commands without stopping to question Him. One of the ways this is learned in military training is through the process of "drill and ceremonies." In other words, you lead the troops on the march and issue commands which they must learn to obey immediately if they want to stay in formation. The Lord used this method with Israel. They learned to obey the cloud and to march as the orders were given by the Lord in this manifestation of His glory.

> *"Whenever the cloud was taken up from above the taber-nacle, the children of Israel would go onward in all their journeys. But if the cloud was not taken up, then they did not journey till the day that it was taken up. For the cloud of the Lord was above the tabernacle by day, and fire was over it by night, in the sight of all the house of Israel, throughout all their journeys."* (Exodus 40:36-38)

HIS PRESENCE WOULD GO WITH THEM

It was not an easy thing to continue to live in the presence of a Holy God! The people still had a rebellious spirit. Instead of walking in faith, they often grumbled and rebelled against the authority of God and His anointed leaders. When adversity came, they quickly wanted to give up and go back to Egypt. Their behavior and attitude eventually wore out even the great patience of the Lord, and He decided not to continue to go with them. He planned to do this so that He would not break out against them in anger. Moses' sincere prayer changed the Lord's mind and He agreed to go with them. Study it again with the revelation you have received from the Lord. As you study it, ask the Lord to allow His Presence to go with you and give you rest!

> *"Then Moses said to the Lord, 'See, You say to me, "'Bring up this people.'" But You have not let me know whom You will send with me. Yet You have said, "'I know you by name, and you have also found grace in My sight.'" Now therefore, I pray, if I have found grace in Your sight, show me now Your way, that I may know You and that I may find grace in Your sight. And consider that this nation is Your people.' And He said, "'My Presence will go with you, and I will give you rest.'"* (Exodus 33:12-14)

85

This is a powerful message to us about the nature of God. We can influence His plans through our sincere prayers of intercession. Your prayers are never ignored by the Lord. He listens and provides for you above and beyond what you ask or imagine. He is faithful and true. He is long suffering, patient, kind, and forgiving. This is a powerful reminder for us that every manifestation of His glory is at the same time a revelation of who He is and what He does. More and more of His attributes become visible and real to us in every encounter with Him. Knowing this and having faith that He is the same yesterday, today and forever, draw near to Him and He will draw near to you. Walk in this trust all the days of your life! He is good and His mercy endures forever and ever! Amen and Amen!

SHOWED HIS GLORY TO MOSES

"So the Lord said to Moses, 'I will also do this thing that you have spoken; for you have found grace in My sight, and I know you by name.' And he said, 'Please, show me Your glory.' Then He said, 'I will make all My goodness pass before you, and I will proclaim the name of the Lord before you. I will be gracious to whom I will be gracious, and I will have compassion on whom I will have compassion.' But He said, 'You cannot see My face; for no man shall see Me, and live.' And the Lord said, 'Here is a place by Me, and you shall stand on the rock. So it shall be, while My glory passes by, that I will put you in the cleft of the rock, and will cover you with My hand while I pass by. Then I will take away My hand, and you shall see My back; but My face shall not be seen.'" (Exodus 33:17-23)

What do you expect when you think of the glory of the Lord coming into your presence? Many people are afraid of His glory. They recognize their sin nature and think of all the times they have "fallen short of His glory." The Lord revealed to Moses that we should not approach Him with this kind of fear. The proper "fear of the Lord" is about deep respect and awe and it always exists in the atmosphere of faith in His attributes of grace and love.

When the Lord revealed His glory to Moses, it was His goodness which He displayed as He spoke of compassion and grace toward His people. You can have full faith in the fact that the Lord is good and He has your best interests at heart. Approach Him in faith and trust in His goodness and grace. He has not changed. His attributes will remain unchanged forever.

FACE TO FACE ENCOUNTERS

"And it came to pass, when Moses entered the tabernacle, that the pillar of cloud descended and stood at the door of the tabernacle, and the Lord talked with Moses. All the people saw the pillar of cloud standing at the tabernacle door, and all the people rose and worshiped, each man in his tent door. So the Lord spoke to Moses face to face, as a man speaks to his friend. And he would return to the camp, but his servant Joshua the son of Nun, a young man, did not depart from the tabernacle." (Exodus 33:9-11)

The Lord continued to meet with Moses, face to face, and Moses lived to tell about it. The Lord spoke directly and audibly to Moses, and this began a process which shattered all of the old fearful images of God which existed from the fall in the Garden to the time of Moses. God is not in a bad mood and He is not planning ways to judge and condemn His people. Remember the words He gave through the prophet Ezekiel (see 18:32) *"For I have no pleasure in the death of one who dies,"* says the Lord God. *"Therefore turn and live!"* In verse 33:11 He took this one step further: *"Say to them: 'As I live,' says the Lord GOD, 'I have no pleasure in the death of the wicked, but that the wicked turn from his way and live. Turn, turn from your evil ways! For why should you die, O house of Israel?'"* Whether wicked or righteous, the Lord does not seek the death of His people. He wants good things for His people and He wants to walk and talk with them as He did with Adam and Eve in the Garden of Eden.

A new relationship has been offered which is much like the old relationship Adam and Eve enjoyed before the fall. Once again men and women can walk and talk with the Lord. Jesus emphasized this in His gospel of the kingdom of God. One example is in John 10:27, *"My sheep hear My voice, and I know them, and they follow Me."* If you are one of His sheep, then you should be hearing His voice and following Him. If you are not hearing His voice, you may want to investigate and find out why this is not happening for you. It may be time to be restored to the kind of relationship which makes you His sheep who hear His voice.

This is the season for us to be walking and talking with the Lord on a daily basis. His glory came down so that you and I could be lifted up, going from glory to glory into the very image of His glory. Look again at 2 Corinthians 3:18, and read it aloud over and over to let it take up residence in your heart: *"But we all, with unveiled face, beholding as in a mirror the glory of the Lord, are being transformed into the same image from glory to glory, just as by the Spirit of the Lord."* The Lord is literally transforming us in spirit and soul so that we can be in His presence and experience His awesome and glorious person.

FORESHADOWED GOD'S PLAN FOR ETERNITY

"Now when these things had been thus prepared, the priests always went into the first part of the tabernacle, performing the services. But into the second part the high priest went alone once a year, not without blood, which he offered for himself and for the people's sins committed in ignorance; the Holy Spirit indicating this, that the way into the Holiest of All was not yet made manifest while the

first tabernacle was still standing. It was symbolic for the present time in which both gifts and sacrifices are offered which cannot make him who performed the service perfect in regard to the conscience—concerned only with foods and drinks, various washings, and fleshly ordinances imposed until the time of reformation." (Hebrews 9:6-10)

As the writer of Hebrews reflects on the time when the glory of the Lord came down and rested on and within His Tabernacle, he points to the prophetic promises released in this manifestation of His presence. The coming of His glory into the Tabernacle was a huge step forward in the process of reconciliation, but the people were still not able to come fully into His presence. This could only happen after the completed work of Christ on the cross. The presence of the glory in the Tabernacle was certainly real for them in their time. However, it was also symbolic and prophetically pointed to the work yet to come. We are so blessed to live after the fulfillment of the requirements of the sacrificial system. We can enter into His glory! We can enter into the Secret Place! We can enter into the Holy of Holies because we are under the blood of Jesus.

"But Christ came as High Priest of the good things to come, with the greater and more perfect tabernacle not made with hands, that is, not of this creation. Not with the blood of goats and calves, but with His own blood He entered the Most Holy Place once for all, having obtained eternal redemption. For if the blood of bulls and goats and the ashes of a heifer, sprinkling the unclean, sanctifies for the purifying of the flesh, how much more shall the blood of Christ, who through the eternal Spirit offered Himself without spot to God, cleanse your conscience from dead works to serve the living God? And for this reason He is the Mediator of the new covenant, by means of death, for the redemption of the transgressions under the first

covenant, that those who are called may receive the promise of the eternal inheritance." (Hebrews 9:11-15)

The things the Lord has done for us are almost too wonderful to believe and accept. How is it that He did all of this for you and me? We need to remember that He also did it for Himself. It was in His heart to restore humanity and call His people back into fellowship with Him. He knew we could never do it for ourselves so He did it all for us in the death and resurrection of Jesus the Christ. But, that is not the end of the story. The Lord has more and more for us. In the passage below, a promise given first through the prophet Amos (verses 9:11-13) was released a second time as the apostles came together to declare the inclusion of Gentile believers with the Jewish members of the Church.

"After this I will return and will rebuild the tabernacle of David, which has fallen down; I will rebuild its ruins, And I will set it up; So that the rest of mankind may seek the Lord, even all the Gentiles who are called by My name, says the Lord who does all these things." (Acts 15:16-17)

All of this was done so that you and I could also seek the Lord and enter into that kind of face to face relationship with Him. All of this was the work of the Lord, and it is marvelous in our sight. The Lord has made the way clear so that He can dwell with us. At the very end of the Bible, this is all declared once more. Note in the passage from Revelation below: *"The tabernacle of God is with men* (mankind: men and women)." He will dwell with us and be our God. We will dwell with Him in His glory and be His people. All the barriers which existed in the past have passed away. Now all things are new! Hallelujah! I feel like shouting out again, "The Lord is good! His mercy endures forever!" Amen and Amen!

"And I heard a loud voice from heaven saying, 'Behold, the tabernacle of God is with men, and He will dwell with them, and they shall be His people. God Himself will be with them and be their God. And God will wipe away every tear from their eyes; there shall be no more death, nor sorrow, nor crying. There shall be no more pain, for the former things have passed away.'" (Revelation 21:3-4)

PRAYER

"Now, my God, may your eyes be open and your ears attentive to the prayers offered in this place. Now arise, O Lord God, and come to your resting place, you and the ark of your might. May your priests, O Lord God, be clothed with salvation, may your saints rejoice in your goodness. O Lord God, do not reject your anointed one." (2 Chronicles 6:40-42a, NIV)

SELAH QUESTIONS

1. What does the teaching in this chapter say about the temple of God in you?

2. Is the Lord sanctifying the temple in you by the presence of His glory? If not, what do you need to do to allow Him to bring this about in your spirit?

3. Are you ready to draw near to Him and to let Him draw near to you (James 4:8)?

4. Can you sense how important it is to the Lord to find a way to tabernacle with His people? List 3-4 specific things this means to you!

5. List some passages from scripture which teach that this is also for you.

CHAPTER 5

LEVEL 4: GLORY ON THE PEOPLE

Everything the Lord does is systematic, orderly and timely. Just at the moment when the need grew strongest, the Lord acted. He had a plan to help Moses with the heavy burden of leading approximately two million people on a forty year journey through the wilderness. However, the plan could only be activated in the appropriate time set by the Lord. Out of His grace, He waited for Moses to ask for help rather than just imposing it on Him. Take note of how these two important things come together to bring the Lord into action.

First, it must be in His time! Then he waits for us to call upon Him to take action on our behalf. Why does the Lord wait for us to ask? Everything in the Kingdom of God works in an orderly manner and in accordance with the authority He establishes. He has given you authority over your assigned area and He doesn't capriciously take it back. He waits for you to exercise your kingdom authority, and then adds His power to it in order to accomplish His purposes. Read aloud several times Psalm 115:16, and let it sink deeply into your heart and mind: *"The heaven, even the heavens, are the Lord's; but the earth He has given to the children of men."*

As with everything else in the Kingdom of God, the progressive release of His glory is orderly and systematic. It progressed from that first release to Moses on the mountain, to the priests, and then it fell upon the Tabernacle. As the glory began to be released by the Lord to the people He started with the leaders. Then it fell upon all the people who were willing to receive it. In all these outpourings of His glory, we see that the Lord is in control and the flow will always be ordered according to His purpose and in His timing.

STARTING WITH THE LEADERS

"So the Lord said to Moses: "Gather to Me seventy men of the elders of Israel, whom you know to be the elders of the people and officers over them; bring them to the tabernacle of meeting, that they may stand there with you. Then I will come down and talk with you there. I will take of the Spirit that is upon you and will put the same upon them; and they shall bear the burden of the people with you, that you may not bear it yourself alone." (Numbers 11:16-17)

As I meditated on this passage, I sought revelation to understand why the Lord took "of the Spirit" that was on Moses to put it on the elders. Why didn't He just give them something separate and new? As I prayed about this, two things came to me from the Spirit. First, I noted that what Moses had was not diminished by this action on the Lord's part. He wasn't left with partial authority, reduced anointing or lesser power. This is a powerful word for you and me about the all sufficiency of the Lord. If we release some of the anointing of the Holy Spirit on our lives and ministries, we will not be left with less. In fact, we will receive more. I believe this is why the Lord said to the disciples, *"Freely you have received, freely give!"* (Matthew 10:8) The Lord has always operated this way. Remember what He said to Abraham,

*"I will make you a great nation; I will bless you and make
your name great; and you shall be a blessing. I will bless
those who bless you, and I will curse him who curses you;
and in you all the families of the earth shall be blessed."*
(Genesis 12:2-3)

The second thing the Holy Spirit revealed to me was that
these men were to carry the same thing Moses carried, but in a
lesser proportion. They were given what they needed to serve
in a smaller area of responsibility. They didn't need all Moses
had, but they needed the same anointing to work on his behalf as
well as on the Lord's behalf. They were being anointed with the
Holy Spirit in order to carry part of Moses' load of responsibilities. Notice also that Moses had been carrying more than what
seventy men could carry. This gives us a better understanding
of the burden Moses was bearing. Can you imagine doing this
when you are over eighty years of age? You would be tired also.
Perhaps you would be exhausted.

*"So Moses went out and told the people the words of the
Lord, and he gathered the seventy men of the elders of
the people and placed them around the tabernacle. Then
the Lord came down in the cloud, and spoke to him, and
took of the Spirit that was upon him, and placed the same
upon the seventy elders; and it happened, when the Spirit
rested upon them, that they prophesied, although they
never did so again."* (Numbers 11:24-25)

The Lord demonstrated that His Spirit/His glory had been
given to them when the Holy Spirit prophesied through them.
They were not given a gift which would be available to them
whenever they wanted to us it. It only happened once, because
it came as a sign to confirm their anointing. Notice also that
another example of God's power to accomplish His purpose
is given in this passage. Two of the selected leaders failed to

appear before the Lord on the mountain. We are not told why they remained in the camp. We can only speculate about what caused them to resist the Lord's calling. But, they didn't escape the outcome.

> *"But two men had remained in the camp: the name of one was Eldad, and the name of the other Medad. And the Spirit rested upon them. Now they were among those listed, but who had not gone out to the tabernacle; yet they prophesied in the camp. And a young man ran and told Moses, and said, 'Eldad and Medad are prophesying in the camp.'"* (Numbers 11:26-27)

The Spirit came on these two at the same time that it fell on the others. Time and distance do not fool the Lord or hinder His spoken Word. When Eldad and Medad prophesied in the camp, it did not set well with Joshua. He had a zeal for the authority of Moses and of the Lord. He was ready to take action against these men, but Moses held him back.

> *"So Joshua the son of Nun, Moses' assistant, one of his choice men, answered and said, "Moses my lord, forbid them!" Then Moses said to him, "Are you zealous for my sake? Oh, that all the Lord's people were prophets and that the Lord would put His Spirit upon them!"* (Numbers 11:28-29)

This incident gives us another picture of the character of Moses. He was not jealous of the anointing on others. In fact, it was His heart's desire for all the people to be prophets and to hear directly from the Lord. As you read the description of this incident in the passages below, compare it with the prophecy given by the Lord in Joel 2:28-32 and restated by Peter in Acts 2:16-21. Then examine your own anointing to validate the prophetic gifting of the Lord in your life and ministry.

GLORY AVAILABLE TO ALL THE PEOPLE

"So they brought what Moses commanded before the tabernacle of meeting. And all the congregation drew near and stood before the Lord. Then Moses said, 'This is the thing which the Lord commanded you to do, and the glory of the Lord will appear to you.'" (Leviticus 9:5-6)

The obedience of the people opened the door for the Lord to bring His glory into the presence of all who were willing to follow Him. The Lord had already released the word prophetically, but it did not manifest until the people stepped out in obedience. Consider these questions: What does obedience have to do with preparing people for the manifestation of God's glory? Does this still apply to you and me today? Can you give an example of this from your own experience?

"Then Aaron lifted his hand toward the people, blessed them, and came down from offering the sin offering, the burnt offering, and peace offerings. And Moses and Aaron went into the tabernacle of meeting, and came out and blessed the people. Then <u>the glory of the Lord appeared to all the people</u>, and fire came out from before the Lord and consumed the burnt offering and the fat on the altar. When all the people saw it, they shouted and fell on their faces. (Leviticus 9:22-24)

This account of the Lord's glory appearing to all the people is filled with vivid imagery and powerful statements about the Lord and the fear and respect it elicits from those who experience it. You have probably read this passage many times and have possibly become very comfortable about it. Read it again, and try to visualize it and experience it yourself for the first time. Imagine yourself standing before the altar when the glory of God appears to you. You see Him with your own eyes and He is awesome and has the appearance of a consuming fire. Then the fire emerges from Him and consumes the offering on the altar. Perhaps you would feel like shouting and falling on your face as the people did that day.

Why is it important for us to consider these things in our day and time? Read the following verse aloud a few times and see if revelation knowledge comes to you. *"But as truly as I live, all the earth shall be filled with the glory of the Lord."* (Numbers 14:21, KJV) Can you picture it? I want to see this with my own eyes. I have a deep desire to see the glory of the Lord fill the whole earth. How about you? Imagine how life on planet Earth might change if we all saw the glory of the Lord? When we see the fire, the power, and the glory of the Lord, His awesome majesty will inspire us to ask what David asked in Psalm 8:4-5:

"What is man that You are mindful of him, and the son of man that You visit him? For You have made him a little lower than the angels (Elohim), and You have crowned him with glory and honor."

I want the entire world to know the Lord God Almighty who appears as a consuming fire and brings everyone to their knees. I want to see everyone on their knees and hear them proclaiming that Jesus Christ is Lord. I desire this because the love of God in me compels me to seek the lost and pray for their salvation. I want everyone to know Him and live with Him forever. Love motivates us to serve Him and seek these things for every man, woman and child on the Earth.

"In God is my salvation and my glory; the rock of my strength, and my refuge, is in God." (Psalm 62:7) As this passage from Psalm 62 affirms, our glory is in the God of glory. Without Him we have no human glory. Tragically, many have exchanged their glory and His glory for cheap imitations. After all the Lord did for them, they still fell back into idolatry in the absence of Moses and his God anointed leadership. Now, they had seventy additional

leaders to carry them through periods like this. However, it is a human tendency to fall away no matter how much the Lord does for us. *"At Horeb they made a calf and worshiped an idol cast from metal. They exchanged their Glory for an image of a bull, which eats grass."* (Psalm 106:19-20, NIV)

"Their Glory" was the Lord, but they didn't know it yet. This is still true today. This is true for every living human being. The Lord created all of us and desires for us to experience His glory and live in His presence forever. We need to make our commitment to Him today and every day. May we daily affirm as the psalmist did: *"O God, my heart is steadfast; I will sing and give praise, even with my glory."* (Psalm 108:1) I am looking for the day of His appearing. How about you?

"Arise, shine; For your light has come! And the glory of the Lord is risen upon you. For behold, the darkness shall cover the earth, and deep darkness the people; But the Lord will arise over you, and His glory will be seen upon you." (Isaiah 60:1-2) (like the glory on Moses?)

ADOPTING THE ATTRIBUTES OF GOD

The more time you spend in the glory the more revelation you receive about the attributes of God. From His first meeting with Moses to this very day, the Lord is revealing more and more of Himself to us. As you continue to spend time with Him and understand Him more fully, you begin to do the things He does and say the things He says. In other words, you begin to adopt the very attributes of God. This was clearly His intent when He created us in His image. We were created to be more and more like Him as we renew our minds and transform our souls. *"But we all, with unveiled face, beholding as in a mirror the glory of the Lord, are being transformed into the same image from glory to glory, just as by the Spirit of the Lord."* (2 Corinthians 3:18)

That is such a powerful thought: *"being transformed into the same image."* It doesn't happen all at once. We go from one experience of His glory to another encounter with His glory, and in the process we are being transformed. We were created in that image, but because of the fall in the Garden we need to be transformed step by step until we reclaim what God intended for us. We should be able to see this happening. Paul says that we should be able to look into a mirror and see it. When you look in a mirror what do you see? Are you seeing the glory of God manifesting on you like it did on Moses? Are you seeing it increase more and more each day? This should be happening. It is God's plan and purpose in your life and your ministry.

One of the important outcomes for us is to be more and more like Him. The glory of human beings is to demonstrate the attributes of God. *"The discretion of a man makes him slow to anger, and his glory is to overlook a transgression."* (Proverbs 19:11) Just as the Lord forgives and covers over our transgressions, we are to be overlooking these same things in others. This is one of the reasons Jesus taught so strongly that we need to forgive as we have been forgiven. When the Lord forgives, He chooses to remember the offense no longer. Thank God that this is one of His powerful attributes. Now we pray that we will be more and more like Him in the church. Can you picture it – a church that forgives, forgets and overlooks every offense? That sounds like heaven, but it is supposed to be that way now even as we pray:

> *"Our Father in heaven, Hallowed be Your name. Your kingdom come. Your will be done On earth as it is in heaven. Give us day by day our daily bread. And forgive us our sins, For we also forgive everyone who is indebted to us. And do not lead us into temptation, But deliver us from the evil one."* (Luke 11:2-4)

As disciples of Jesus Christ, we are striving to imitate Him in every possible way. It may be difficult to imagine this in your own life and more difficult to see it in others. You may wonder how you can do such things as these. Can you ever have this kind of glory? Is it right for you to seek it and to ask for it? As you consider these questions, remember that Jesus has already prayed for it and paid for it. Consider carefully what Jesus meant when He prayed the following prayer. Did He really mean it? If so, then receive it and live in it! Amen?

"And the glory which You gave Me I have given them, that they may be one just as We are one: I in them, and You in Me; that they may be made perfect in one, and that the world may know that You have sent Me, and have loved them as You have loved Me." (John 17:22-23)

If you are struggling with these concepts, it is okay! But, don't stay in this spiritual place of doubt for very long. Always seek more revelation, wisdom, understanding, and counsel from the Holy Spirit. Speak these passages aloud over and over until they become your very own decrees in agreement with God. The world doesn't understand this, because it has not been given to them to fully grasp it. But, you have been given the Spirit of truth who will guide you into all truth. Meditate on the passage below!

"But we speak the wisdom of God in a mystery, the hidden wisdom which God ordained before the ages for our glory, which none of the rulers of this age knew; for had they known, they would not have crucified the Lord of glory." (1 Corinthians 2:7-8)

PROGRESSIVE REVELATION OF WHO HE IS

1. HIS GLORY BROUGHT PROVISION

Through His provision, the Lord revealed to the people what He had spoken to Moses. His glory truly is seen in His goodness. The Lord became their strong provider in every area of need. He gave them bread (manna), meat (quail), and water. His provision was often supernatural and beyond human explanation. Bread came down from Heaven. *"Yet He had commanded the clouds above, And opened the doors of heaven, Had rained down manna on them to eat, And given them of the bread of heaven. Men ate angels' food; He sent them food to the full."* (Psalm 78:23-25) Winds brought vast numbers of quail and dropped them at their feet. The Lord even caused water to flow from a rock when they were thirsty. *"The people asked, and He brought quail, and satisfied them with the bread of heaven. He opened the rock, and water gushed out; It ran in the dry places like a river."* (Psalm 105:40-41) In all of these things, the Lord was revealing powerful things about Himself and how He expected them to live. Reflect on these things and apply them to your own spiritual walk with the Lord.

> *"So He humbled you, allowed you to hunger, and fed you with manna which you did not know nor did your fathers know, that He might make you know that man shall not live by bread alone; but man lives by every word that proceeds from the mouth of the Lord. Your garments did not wear out on you, nor did your foot swell these forty years."* (Deuteronomy 8:3-4)

Reflecting on all the Lord has done for his people, the psalmist wrote, *"We have thought, O God, on Your loving kindness, in the midst of Your temple."* (Psalm 48:9) When we reflect on the goodness of God, which continues to be revealed in His glory, we too need to remember all He has done. When we remember all these things, we cannot resist giving Him praise, honor, and glory for His goodness to us. During the time of restoring the walls of Jerusalem and the worship of the Lord in the restored Temple, Nehemiah said, "*You also gave Your good Spirit to instruct them, and did not withhold Your manna from their mouth, and gave them water for their thirst.*" (Nehemiah 9:20)

This is a good time for you to stop for a moment and reflect on all that the Lord has provided for you. As you remember the many times when He has fed you, healed you, inspired you, blessed you, and favored you, begin to release praise and glory to Him. With a renewed and deeper sense of gratitude for these specific things, praise Him with all of your heart, all of your soul, and all of your might. Praise Him for all He has done, all He is doing, and all He has promised to do for you in the future. He is your source for all good and perfect gifts. Jesus taught that He still provides the bread of Heaven for you.

"*Our fathers ate the manna in the desert; as it is written, 'He gave them bread from heaven to eat.'*" Then Jesus said to them, "*Most assuredly, I say to you, Moses did not give you the bread from heaven, but My Father gives you the true bread from heaven. For the bread of God is He who comes down from heaven and gives life to the world.*" (John 6:31-33)

2. HIS GLORY WAS THEIR PROTECTIVE SHIELD

"*And the Angel of God, who went before the camp of Israel, moved and went behind them; and the pillar of cloud went from before them and stood behind them. So it came between the camp of the Egyptians and the camp of Israel. Thus it was a cloud and darkness to the one, and it gave light by night to the other, so that the one did not come near the other all that night.*" (Exodus 14:19-20)

103

As Israel fled from Pharaoh, the glory presence of the Lord was visible to them in the "pillar of cloud." They could see the glory of the Lord with their own eyes. By day, it looked like a cloud and by night it looked like a column of fire. When they were in danger, the pillar of cloud and the Angel of God stood between them and their enemies. Look carefully at the explanation Moses gave to the people, *"And Moses said to the people, "Do not be afraid. Stand still, and see the salvation of the Lord, which He will accomplish for you today. For the Egyptians whom you see today, you shall see again no more forever. The Lord will fight for you, and you shall hold your peace."* (Exodus 14:13-14) He did all of this for their salvation, and He will do the same for you.

The good news is that the same God who protected them will protect you. He is the same yesterday, today, and forever. He will not desert you or leave you as an orphan. He is your strong protector and your shield in all the battles you face in this present time of spiritual warfare. Begin to reflect on how the Lord has been your shield and protector in the past. As you do this, let it build up your faith in what He will do for you in the future. Meditating on Psalm 91 is a great way to pause and think about Who the Lord is and what He has promised for you.

"You shall not be afraid of the terror by night, nor of the arrow that flies by day, nor of the pestilence that walks in darkness, nor of the destruction that lays waste at noonday. A thousand may fall at your side, and ten thousand at your right hand; But it shall not come near you. Only with your eyes shall you look, and see the reward of the wicked. Because you have made the Lord, who is my refuge, even the Most High, your dwelling place, no evil shall befall you, nor shall any plague come near your dwelling; For He shall give His angels charge over you, to keep you in all your ways." (Psalm 91:5-11)

3. THE GLORY WAS THE RIGHTEOUS JUDGE

"Moses took his tent and pitched it outside the camp, far from the camp, and called it the tabernacle of meeting. And it came to pass that everyone who sought the Lord went out to the tabernacle of meeting which was outside the camp. So it was, whenever Moses went out to the tabernacle, that all the people rose, and each man stood at his tent door and watched Moses until he had gone into the tabernacle." (Exodus 33:7-8)

People who do not know the Lord may be frightened by the thought of Him being their judge. However, when you spend time in His presence, you get to know Him better as He reveals more and more of His attributes to you. He is righteous and holy, and He is also long suffering, kind, gracious, merciful, and forgiving. He does not desire to see us die for our sins. His desire is for us to return to Him and to let Him restore us in spirit, soul, and body. He has done everything necessary for our healing, redemption, restoration, and righteousness. Remember that the word righteous means to have a right relationship with Him. You cannot make that happen, but the good news is that He has already done it for you in the death and resurrection of Jesus Christ. Embrace Him as your righteous judge knowing what He has done for you and continues to provide to this very day. Seek the glory of God and let Him establish you once more in His righteousness. Then join with the psalmist in giving Him praise for who He is.

"The Lord executes righteousness and justice for all who are oppressed. He made known His ways to Moses, His acts to the children of Israel. The Lord is merciful and gracious, Slow to anger, and abounding in mercy." (Psalm 103:6-8)

105

4. JUDGMENT FOR GRUMBLING AND COMPLAINING

"So Moses and Aaron said to all the Israelites, 'in the evening you will know that it was the Lord who brought you out of Egypt, and in the morning you will see the glory of the Lord, because he has heard your grumbling against him. Who are we, that you should grumble against us?' Moses also said, 'You will know that it was the Lord when he gives you meat to eat in the evening and all the bread you want in the morning, because he has heard your grumbling against him. Who are we? You are not grumbling against us, but against the Lord.'" (Exodus 16:6-8)

Spending time in the glory helps us to understand more and more about the relationship we have with the Lord. It is a covenant relationship. The Lord offers us far more than He asks of us. Some people see Him as the one who is always there to answer all their prayers and serve all their needs. He does so much for us, but we must remember that He is the Creator and we are His creation. He is the Master and we are His servants. He is the teacher and we are His students. The anointed priests understood this relationship. They always went in to His presence in order to minister to Him.

In the glory, we learn again the spiritual concept of "the fear of the Lord." It is not about being so afraid of Him that you live in terror and dread. The fear of the Lord is about a deep respect for Who He is and an acknowledgement of who we are in Him. We serve Him and we are called to minister to Him as part of the kingdom of priests established through the completed work of Jesus Christ. This does not give us the right to grumble and complain about Him every time we feel that we are in need. Grumbling and complaining have never been acceptable in His sight. Even if we did not receive anything else from Him, He has already done enough for us. As you think on these things notice the difference between how Moses complained and how the people complained. The people complained about God to one another. Moses, on the other hand, complained to God in prayer, and the Lord answered his prayers and gave him more blessing and favor.

> *"The voice of the Lord makes the deer give birth, and strips the forests bare; and in His temple everyone says, "Glory!" The Lord sat enthroned at the Flood, and the Lord sits as King forever. The Lord will give strength to His people; The Lord will bless His people with peace."* (Psalm 29:9)

5. HE NOW DWELLS AMONG HIS PEOPLE

> *"I will dwell among the children of Israel and will be their God. And they shall know that I am the Lord their God, who brought them up out of the land of Egypt, that I may dwell among them. I am the Lord their God."* (Exodus 29:45-46)

It is an awesome thing to have the Creator God dwelling in our midst. It is always amazing and wonderful to experience His presence when the glory comes. The good news for you and me is that He has extended this promise to us. Look again at what Jesus taught in John chapters fourteen through seventeen. Over and over, He tells us that His desire is to dwell in us. Notice also that all these promises are prefaced by the statement of Jesus, "If you obey." With this in mind, look again at Exodus 25:8, *"And let them make Me a sanctuary, that I may dwell among them."*

Some say the promises made by Jesus were only for the disciples who were with Him at that time, but look again at the Lord's words in John 17:20-21, *"I do not pray for these alone, but also for those who will believe in Me through their*

*word; that they all may be one, as You, Father, are in Me, and
I in You; that they also may be one in Us, that the world may
believe that You sent Me."* All of these promises and blessings
are for you because you have believed in Him. The Tabernacle
and Temple are gone, but the promises remain forever. Now the
temple is in you: *"Do you not know that you are the temple of
God and that the Spirit of God dwells in you?"* (1 Corinthians
3:16) Remember that all the promises of God are eternal and
will be valid forever for all His people.

*"Moreover I will make a covenant of peace with them,
and it shall be an everlasting covenant with them; I
will establish them and multiply them, and I will set My
sanctuary in their midst forevermore. My tabernacle also
shall be with them; indeed I will be their God, and they
shall be My people."* (Ezekiel 37:26-27)

PRAYER

*"And this I pray, that your love may abound still more and
more in knowledge and all discernment, that you may
approve the things that are excellent, that you may be sincere and without offense till the day of Christ, being filled
with the fruits of righteousness which are by Jesus Christ,
to the glory and praise of God."* (Philippians 1:9-11)

SELAH QUESTIONS

1. Give two reasons why the Lord took of the Spirit on Moses to anoint the leaders rather than just giving them something new.

2. What does obedience have to do with preparing people for the manifestation of God's glory?

3. Since the Tabernacle and Temple are gone, where does the Lord dwell now?

4. List at least four of the attributes of God which have been revealed to you, and explain how these relate to experiencing His glory.
   a.
   b.
   c.
   d.

5. How should you change your lifestyle in order to better host the glory of God?

CHAPTER 6

LEVEL 5: GLORY IN THE TEMPLE

———*ೲ*———

Y ou can learn a great deal about hosting the glory from the Biblical accounts of the building, dedication, and services of the Temple. For the first time, the glory rested in a permanent structure. In the past, the Tabernacle of His presence moved with the people. Now the people came to this place where the glory of the Lord rested. This represented a major shift in how the people would relate to the Lord. It also represented another level in the fulfillment of His promise to dwell among His people. The Lord was keeping every aspect of His portion of the covenant which He made with their ancestors and later extended to them.

The Lord made His presence known by letting His glory come down in a vivid visual display and demonstrating that in His presence no man or woman could stand. In the full manifestation of His power, the priests were powerless to continue their work. For the first time in centuries, the cloud of His presence was visible to all the people. When He occupied the Temple, He made a clear statement of approval for their work and the desires of their heart to be close to Him. They had done a great deal of work to cleanse the Temple and consecrate it, but it was the presence of His glory which truly made it holy. As you read and reflect on the beautiful description of the coming of His glory, try to visualize it and make it part of your own experience of His indwelling presence.

> *"And it came to pass when the priests came out of the Most Holy Place (for all the priests who were present had sanctified themselves, without keeping to their divisions), and the Levites who were the singers, all those of Asaph and Heman and Jeduthun, with their sons and their brethren, stood at the east end of the altar, clothed in white linen, having cymbals, stringed instruments and harps, and with them one hundred and twenty priests sounding with trumpets—indeed it came to pass, when the trumpeters and singers were as one, to make __one sound__ to be heard in praising and thanking the Lord, and when they lifted up their voice with the trumpets and cymbals and instruments of music, and praised the Lord, saying: "For He is good, For His mercy endures forever," that the house, the house of the Lord, was filled with a cloud, so that the priests could not continue ministering because of the cloud; for the glory of the Lord filled the house of God.* (2 Chronicles 5:11-14)

GLORY CAME IN RESPONSE TO UNITY

The passage above from 2 Chronicles says that all of the people singing and playing different types of musical instruments made "one sound." How is that possible? Think about it! There were 120 priests blowing shofars, musicians playing numerous types of stringed instruments and sounding cymbals, and the Levitical singers sang with all their hearts. If you have heard multiple shofars being sounded at the same time, you know that each one has a unique sound and you can hear many different sounds at the same time. In addition, the other instruments and singers would obviously make many more different kinds of sounds. So, how did they all make "one sound" that day?

111

I believe that the words "one sound" refer to the spirit of unity present among the people at the time of the dedication of the Temple. They had a common purpose and shared the same basic goals as a nation and as a household of faith. For the first time since leaving Egypt, they were in an extended period of peace with neighboring nations. There was unity in the royal family and in the royal courts of the nation. The people saw the wisdom of King Solomon and were still impressed by the way the Lord was working through Him. Everything seemed to come together in unity to make this moment in their history possible.

It is rare to get so many people to come together in unity. We rarely see a family in true unity much less a city, state, or nation. Yet, this is one of the most powerful things we can do to bring the glory of God and live in His blessing and favor. There is great spiritual power in unity and agreement. Even a small group in agreement can release the awesome power of God to accomplish great things in the Kingdom of God. Jesus said, *"Again I say to you that if two of you agree on earth concerning anything that they ask, it will be done for them by My Father in heaven. For where two or three are gathered together in My name, I am there in the midst of them."* (Matthew 18:19-20) It is time for us to be elevated to the level of "whatever" so that whatever we ask in His name will be done. This only happens when we stand together in unity and agreement.

THE GLORY DID NOT COME
WHEN DAVID DID THE SAME THINGS

During the reign of David, there was very little national unity. If it came, it only lasted for short periods of time. Over and over in the stories about David we see what looks like the beginning of unity, but it never lasts for very long. When the tribal leaders of Israel came to him at Hebron to make him king, it looked like they were finally coming together as one. *"All these men of war, who could keep ranks, came to Hebron with a loyal heart, to make David king over all Israel; and all the rest of Israel were of one mind to make David king.*" (1 Chronicles 12:38) However, a strong rebellious spirit still thrived in Israel.

> "*And there happened to be there a rebel, whose name was Sheba the son of Bichri, a Benjamite. And he blew a trumpet, and said: "We have no share in David, Nor do we have inheritance in the son of Jesse; Every man to his tents, O Israel!" So every man of Israel deserted David, and followed Sheba the son of Bichri. But the men of Judah, from the Jordan as far as Jerusalem, remained loyal to their king.*" (2 Samuel 20:1-2)

Almost as soon as it started the unity of the kingdom fell apart. Everyone wanted to do what was right in their own heart rather than follow David. This was in reality rebellion against God, because they refused to follow the leadership and submit to the authority of God's anointed servant. They preferred to select and anoint their own kings rather than accepting the ones the Lord chose for them. People are the same today. We have not learned the lessons of history very well, and as a result we repeat the same personal and national mistakes.

We are living in a time of rebellion and amongst a rebellious people. It is so rare to see groups of believers of any size standing in unity and agreement. As a result, we have not hosted the glory of God very well. I hear a call of the Lord for us to break free from the spirit of rebellion and come together in unity so that we can experience more of His glory and live as His loyal followers. Can you hear that call? I pray that more and more of us will hear the call and lay down our own plans and desires as we take up His. Imagine the power and authority that will be released when this happens.

There was no unity within David's own house. His son, Absalom, rebelled and tried to steal the nation away from David's control. "*Then Absalom sent spies throughout all the tribes of*

Israel, saying, "As soon as you hear the sound of the trumpet, then you shall say, 'Absalom reigns in Hebron!'" (2 Samuel 15:10) David's wife, Michal, was against him. As King Saul had planned and predicted, she was a constant thorn in David's side. She tried to turn every victory into failure and ridiculed his devotion to the Lord.

> *"Then David returned to bless his household. And Michal the daughter of Saul came out to meet David, and said, "How glorious was the king of Israel today, uncovering himself today in the eyes of the maids of his servants, as one of the base fellows shamelessly uncovers himself!"* (2 Samuel 6:20)

The rebellion and disunity in David's house did not end here. His son, Adonijah, made himself king while David was still alive. He won the hearts of the people, Joab, the army commander and Abiathar the priest. They joined him in his rebellious attempt to take the throne of David for himself. Notice again that all these people made their own choices rather than accepting the one anointed by the Lord. The Lord had chosen Solomon, but the people jumped ahead of God's plan to make Adonijah king while David was still living.

> *"Then Adonijah the son of Haggith exalted himself, saying, "I will be king"; and he prepared for himself chariots and horsemen, and fifty men to run before him. (And his father had not rebuked him at any time by saying, "Why have you done so?"* (1 Kings 1:5-6a)

Why was all of this happening? Sin had opened the door for disunity and rebellion. David's sin in the matter of Bathsheba and the planned death of her husband, Uriah the Hittite, brought the judgment of God on the household of David. In addition, Joab, the commander of the army, did what he wanted to do rather than following the desires of King David. In Joab's later years, there was murder, deception, and rebellion in the army. Joab murdered anyone who was a threat to his position, and was easily persuaded to enter into a rebellion against the Lord's anointed. It is no small wonder that the glory of God did not appear in the midst of all this turmoil, disunity, rebellion, and open sin.

NEHEMIAH DID WHAT SOLOMON DID BUT THE GLORY DID NOT MANIFEST

There was no unity with the people or the government officials during the time when Ezra, the priest restored the Temple and Nehemiah, the governor, rebuilt the walls of Jerusalem. When they dedicated the Temple, they followed the same pattern used by Solomon at the first ceremony, but the glory of God did not appear. Why? The people had disobeyed the Lord and intermarried with the Gentiles in the land. They had started to worship the idols of these groups and turned away from the Lord. When Ezra and Nehemiah came to restore things, these individuals did not support them because of their mixed loyalties.

Even the priests were not loyal to Nehemiah or to God. The High Priest, Eliashib, had intermarried and supported the enemies of Israel rather than the new leaders the Lord brought to them. He was actually married into the family of one of Israel's worst enemies, Tobiah. Eliashib had removed everything from the treasuries of the Temple and turned it into a place for Tobiah to live. Even though Eliashib was the first mentioned in Nehemiah, Chapter Three, to start rebuilding the wall, he was disloyal and a threat to the completion of the work on the wall. Later, his rebellion became intolerable and he had to be removed from office.

"Now before this, Eliashib the priest, having authority over the storerooms of the house of our God, was allied with Tobiah. And he had prepared for him a large room,

where previously they had stored the grain offerings, the frankincense, the articles, the tithes of grain, the new wine and oil, which were commanded to be given to the Levites and singers and gatekeepers, and the offerings for the priests." (Nehemiah 13:4-5)

The Glory did not come into the midst of all of this turmoil, rebellion, disunity, and disloyalty. Rebellion and disunity do not create an environment which the Lord will bless with His presence. Throughout the teachings of the Torah, the writings, the prophets, and the New Testament, the Lord has made known how He values unity and agreement. In the passage below, reflect on this teaching from the writer of Proverbs. All of these "abominations" were present among the people. For this reason they failed to attract the presence of the Lord. What does this say to you about hosting the glory?

"These six things the Lord hates, Yes, seven are an abomination to Him: a proud look, a lying tongue, hands that shed innocent blood, a heart that devises wicked plans, feet that are swift in running to evil, a false witness who speaks lies, and one who sows discord among brethren." (Proverbs 6:16-19)

ONE MAJOR PURPOSE OF THE TEMPLE WAS TO PROMOTE UNITY

"When Solomon had finished praying, fire came down from heaven and consumed the burnt offering and the sacrifices; and the glory of the Lord filled the temple. And the priests could not enter the house of the Lord, because the glory of the Lord had filled the Lord's house. When all the children of Israel saw how the fire came down, and the glory of the Lord on the temple, they bowed their faces to the ground on the pavement, and worshiped and

praised the Lord, saying: "For He is good, For His mercy endures forever." (2 Chronicles 7:1-3)

The Lord gave a powerful demonstration of the impact of our agreement and unity. I want to suggest again that you try to visualize all of these things and apply them to your own ministry and your plans to attract the glory of God. Strong visual imagery provides lasting memories. The Lord created us to learn and retain information in this way. It is no surprise that He would use this gift to teach us profound things about the kingdom of God and the keys to hosting His presence.

When you combine the lessons from the passage above with the accounts of the building of the Tabernacle, the Tent of David, and the restored Temple, you will see that the Lord is giving you a clear message about the power of unity and agreement. It literally opens the door for the release of His power to accomplish great things through our service in the Kingdom. The first lesson from their experiences is about getting into agreement with one another. This is rare but possible. Remember how often Jesus taught this same principle. When only two to three come into agreement it releases the awesome power of God to accomplish His purposes in our lives.

The second lesson is about getting into agreement and unity with God. When you get into agreement with God, just imagine the power you bring to support the things you have released through the authority He has given you. How can you get into agreement with the Lord? The entire Bible is given to you as a guidebook for agreement. Study the Word of God and learn all the lessons about the things which have been clearly revealed as the will of God. When you agree with the Word of God and the will of God, you are in a right relationship to attract His glory and release His power. The Lord taught this directly to Solomon.

"Then the word of the Lord came to Solomon, saying: "Concerning this temple which you are building, if you

117

walk in My statutes, execute My judgments, keep all My commandments, and walk in them, then I will perform My word with you, which I spoke to your father David. And I will dwell among the children of Israel, and will not forsake My people Israel." (1 Kings 6:11-13)

GLORY IN THE TEMPLE CAUSED RIVAL NATIONS TO FEAR

God's presence in the temple caused rival nations to fear Him and his anointed leaders and servants. How would you like for all your enemies to fear Him and stop every attack on you, your family, your business, and your church? That sounds good doesn't it? It can happen! The Lord has revealed the way to make this work. He taught it in a very profound way through the work of Solomon and the people of Israel when they built the Temple. Preparing a place for Him to dwell with you attracts His presence. When He comes, all of His power is available to His people. Study the passage below and make a list of all the benefits the Lord's presence brought to them during that period of time.

"For he had dominion over all the region on this side of the River from Tiphsah even to Gaza, namely over all the kings on this side of the River; and he had peace on every side all around him. And Judah and Israel dwelt safely, each man under his vine and his fig tree, from Dan as far as Beersheba, all the days of Solomon." (1 Kings 4:24-25)

It is one thing to think about Solomon having dominion over the regions around Israel, but what does this have to do with you? Think about what the Lord intended in the creation when His Word says, *"Then God said, 'Let Us make man in Our image, according to Our likeness; let them have dominion over the fish*

118

of the sea, over the birds of the air, and over the cattle, over all the earth and over every creeping thing that creeps on the earth.'" (Genesis 1:26) According to this passage, God created all human beings to have "dominion" over all the things around them. In what ways can you have dominion over things around you?

The second powerful message is about living in peace. Do you need a little more peace (shalom of God) in your life? Host the glory and allow the Lord to release it into your own heart and establish it for you, your family, and your church. I want to have *"peace on every side all around"* like Solomon enjoyed. How about you? This peace or "Shalom" of God also caused the people to live safely in the land and allowed them to do their work without enemy attacks. I want that too! How about you?

> *"For thus says the LORD of hosts: 'Once more (it is a little while) I will shake heaven and earth, the sea and dry land; and I will shake all nations, and they shall come to the Desire of All Nations, and I will fill this temple with glory,' says the LORD of hosts".* (Haggai 2:6-7)

Be prepared for it. The glory of God is returning to his temple. But where is this temple? The Temple in Jerusalem is gone. Yet, the Lord is promising to bring His glory back into the temple. *"Do you not know that you are the temple of God and that the Spirit of God dwells in you? If anyone defiles the temple of God, God will destroy him. For the temple of God is holy, which temple you are".* (1 Corinthians 3:16-17) Are you ready for the glory to manifest in this temple which is in you? Are you ready for the Lord to release His peace, provision, protection, and prosperity through your temple? Imagine how glorious this can be. Then study the passage below and apply it to this promise of the Lord.

> *"'The glory of this latter temple shall be greater than the former,' says the Lord of hosts. 'And in this place I will give peace,' says the Lord of hosts".* (Haggai 2:9)

All of these promises have been given to you and me as well as to those who first heard them. All of this can be ours. We can hold on to it until the time is fulfilled and the Lord comes to dwell with us permanently in the New Heaven and the New Earth. What we experience now foreshadows this time which the Lord promises to bring to us. At that time there will be no need for a building called a Temple, because the Lord will dwell in us and we will dwell in Him. Remember what John wrote in Revelation 21:22-23, *"But I saw no temple in it, for the Lord God Almighty and the Lamb are its temple. The city had no need of the sun or of the moon to shine in it, for the glory of God illuminated it. The Lamb is its light."*

Until that time comes, we have this temple established in us. Like the Temple of old, the Lord wants to manifest His glory in us and through us. He has come down from Heaven to dwell with His people. He has fulfilled what Jesus promised and prayed (John chapters 14 through 17). Now picture the glory coming into you and try to visualize it like the description in Revelation 15:8, *"The temple was filled with smoke from the glory of God and from His power, and no one was able to enter the temple till the seven plagues of the seven angels were completed."* Are you ready for it?

PRAYER

"For this reason I bow my knees to the Father of our Lord Jesus Christ, from whom the whole family in heaven and earth is named, that He would grant you, according to the riches of His glory, to be strengthened with might through His Spirit in the inner man, that Christ may dwell in your hearts through faith; that you, being rooted and grounded in love, may be able to comprehend with all the saints what is the width and length and depth and height—to know the love of Christ which passes knowledge; that you may be filled with all the fullness of God." **(Ephesians 3:14-19)**

SELAH QUESTIONS

1. What is the key to hosting the glory of God revealed in the Temple?

2. How does this apply to you in this present time?

3. What can you do to better host the glory of God?

4. What benefits should you expect from His dwelling in you?

5. Summarize the teachings of Jesus about God dwelling in you which are given in the Gospel of John, chapters fourteen through seventeen.

CHAPTER 7

LEVEL 6: GLORY IN THE PERSON OF YESHUA

———*∾∾∾*———

"Lift up your heads, O you gates! And be lifted up, you everlasting doors! And the King of glory shall come in. Who is this King of glory? The Lord strong and mighty, the Lord mighty in battle. Lift up your heads, O you gates! Lift up, you everlasting doors! And the King of glory shall come in. Who is this King of glory? The Lord of hosts, He is the King of glory." (Psalm 24:7-10)

David raised a very important question in Psalm 24, "Who is this King of glory?" This is a question each of us will be required to answer personally one day in the not too distant future. There is also a very important reason why you need to deal with this question right now. Without getting the answer to this question, you will not be able to experience the fullness of the glory of God. The glory is not about angels, miracles, signs or wonders. It is about Him. It is about Father God and our Lord, Jesus the Christ. He is the King of Glory! We must always keep our focus on the Lord even when angels appear. Angels appear as directed by God, and come to us as ministering spirits. They minister in ways which bring glory to the Lord. When the gospel of the kingdom is preached and when the glory appears, we will see healings, miracles, signs and wonders, but all of these are given in order to confirm the gospel and to direct our attention back on the Lord of glory. *"Let us fix our eyes on Jesus, the author and perfecter of our faith,"* (Hebrews 12:2a, NIV)

The Hebrew word "kabod" appears at least 148 times in the Bible and is translated as glory. The root meaning of the word "kabod" is heavy. When it is translated as "glory," it means the heavy or weighty presence of the Lord Himself. At this point you might ask whether the "kabod" (glory) refers to the presence of God or of Jesus. The answer is both! Study carefully the revelation given in the first six verses of the book of Hebrews.

> *"God, who at various times and in various ways spoke in time past to the fathers by the prophets, has in these last days spoken to us by His Son, whom He has appointed heir of all things, through whom also He made the worlds; who <u>being the brightness of His glory</u> and the <u>express image of His person</u>, and upholding all things by the word of His power, when He had by Himself purged our sins, sat down at the right hand of the Majesty on high, having become so much better than the angels, as He has by inheritance obtained a more excellent name than they. For to which of the angels did He ever say: 'You are My Son, today I have begotten You'? And again: 'I will be to Him a Father, and He shall be to Me a Son'? But when He again brings the firstborn into the world, He says: 'Let all the angels of God worship Him.'"* (Hebrews 1:1-6)

Jesus is the "brightness of His glory" and the "express image of His person." When the "King of Glory" comes into our midst, we should feel the weight (kabod) of His presence. John said it this way, *"And the Word became flesh and dwelt among us, and we beheld His glory, the glory as of the only begotten of the Father, full of grace and truth."* (John 1:14) I believe that John is making a reference to his experience on the mountain as recorded in Matthew 17:1-2, *"Now after six days Jesus took Peter, James, and John his brother, led them up on a high mountain by themselves; and He was transfigured before them. His face shone like the sun, and His clothes became as white as the light."* These three disciples were the inner circle among the followers of Jesus. They were given the unique privilege of seeing the glory of God radiating from the person of Jesus.

Something new and awesome was revealed when the Lord moved the glory one step closer to His people. In the previous levels of glory, we understand that the glory rested on or in people and places. The Bible speaks of it resting on a mountain, on the priests, in a tabernacle, on the people, and in the Temple. In this sixth level of the manifestation of His glory, the Lord introduces something completely new. The glory of God is the person of Jesus Christ. *"For in Him dwells all the fullness of the Godhead bodily;"* (Colossians 2:9) The glory is not just in Him to a limited degree. All of the fullness is in Him. It is not just on Him temporarily as we previously saw in those anointed for a particular task. It is Him! *"For it pleased the Father that in Him all the fullness should dwell,"* (Colossians 1:19) Earlier this year, the Lord gave me a better understanding of this truth in a vision.

(Vision: Wednesday, January 23, 2013)

As I went into His presence, I saw something like a very huge Bible open before me. It seemed to be on fire and the Glory of the Lord was radiating out from it. I saw this once before, but this morning I didn't recall the message that went with the previous vision. As I thought about this, I heard the Lord say, "Everything you do today should be based on the Word!" We all know this, so I assumed that there must be something more to this message from the Lord. Then the Lord began to release a series of visions in which I saw Him providing for many different people in a variety of places around the world. These people were each receiving exactly what they needed and no two were receiving the same thing.

Then it came to me! The only way we can step fully into this flow of provision is to base everything on the Word of God. If you need provision, ask for it in accordance with the Word. This was another reminder of how important it is in this season to have the Word of God stored in our hearts. We cannot step out of the flow and go to another place to look up something in the Bible. We need to have it readily at hand so that we can immediately stand in agreement and receive what the Lord has for us. What do you need from the Lord today? Can you find it in the Word? Then go to that part of the Word and place a claim on the promises of God released to you in that passage. After you have made this claim, begin to confess it as if you have already received it. Confess it over and over until it manifests. So much is available today, and it is all based on His Word.

Then I heard the Lord say, "The Word is My Glory!" We may not all understand this message from the Lord. How is His Word and His Glory the same thing? I know that His Word brings Him glory! I know that His Word teaches about His glory! I know that when we act on His Word it brings glory to Him! But, the Lord is now saying that His Glory and His Word are the same thing. Then it came to me by the Holy Spirit. The Word I was seeing this morning was the "Living Word!" It was a spiritual manifestation and representation of the Lord Jesus who came as the glory filled and glory radiating image of God's Word. Everything is based on the Living Word which is Jesus Christ. I was then led to two very powerful scriptures:

"In the past God spoke to our forefathers through the prophets at many times and in various ways, but in these last days he has spoken to us by his Son, whom he appointed heir of all things, and through whom he made the universe. The Son is the radiance of God's glory and

125

*the exact representation of his being, sustaining all things
by his powerful word."* (Hebrews 1:1-3a, NIV)

Jesus is *"the radiance of God's Glory!"* He is not merely
carrying the glory of God. He is the Glory! He is *"the exact
representation of his being"*! He sustains everything by His
powerful Word. Today and every day we must base everything
we do on this powerful truth and upon Him as our Lord and
Savior. Yeshua ha Messiach is the Glory of God! Our one true
foundation is the living Word of God.

*"For no one can lay any foundation other than the one
already laid, which is Jesus Christ. If any man builds on
this foundation using gold, silver, costly stones, wood, hay
or straw, his work will be shown for what it is, because
the Day will bring it to light. It will be revealed with fire,
and the fire will test the quality of each man's work. If
what he has built survives, he will receive his reward. If
it is burned up, he will suffer loss; he himself will be
saved, but only as one escaping through the flames."* (1
Corinthians 3:11-15, NIV)

Everything is based and founded on the person and work of
Jesus Christ. If we want to flow in the fullness of what the Lord
has for us, we must be firmly established on this foundation.
If you want to experience the glory of the Lord, you must be
founded on Jesus! If you want the provisions He has for you,
you must base it on the Living Word of God! May you step into
the flow today! Amen and Amen!

(End of Vision)

GLORY OF GOD APPEARED AS YESHUA

This revelation that Jesus is the glory of God is not something which the Lord just suddenly released as a surprise for us. It was actually foreshadowed long ago through the prophets. The Lord had a glorious plan which seemed to be almost too good to be true. No one knew how this was possible, but their hearts longed to see the day of its appearing. One of the most clear prophetic words about the coming of the glory of God in Yeshua ha Messiach came through the prophet Isaiah. The words given through the prophet made it clear that the revealing of God's glory in this manner would change everything in our world including the land itself. This is a powerful spiritual reality, and I pray that the Lord will give you wisdom and revelation to more fully understand it.

"Comfort, yes, comfort My people!" Says your God. "Speak comfort to Jerusalem, and cry out to her, that her warfare is ended, that her iniquity is pardoned; for she has received from the Lord's hand double for all her sins." The voice of one crying in the wilderness: "Prepare the way of the Lord; Make straight in the desert a highway for our God. Every valley shall be exalted and every mountain and hill brought low; The crooked places shall be made straight and the rough places smooth; The glory of the Lord shall be revealed, and all flesh shall see it together; For the mouth of the Lord has spoken." (Isaiah 40:1-5)

This prophetic word gives us a great reminder that nothing the Lord does is by accident or merely in response to what is happening in the world. The plans and purposes of God transcend the things in this world. In the Lord's timing all things will happen as He has pre-determined. From the beginning, the Lord knew all of the methods and means He would use to bring His glory down to dwell with us and within us. To help us understand His plan, He released prophetic messages for us centuries before it manifested. *"For this One has been counted worthy of more glory than Moses, inasmuch as He who built the house has more honor than the house."* (Hebrews 3:3)

On the Mount of Transfiguration, some truly amazing and wonderful things were experienced by Peter, James, and John. In addition to the awesome glory appearance of Jesus, they saw two very significant prophetic people from the past. We read in Mark 9:4, *"And Elijah appeared to them with Moses, and they were talking with Jesus."* Can you imagine seeing Elijah and Moses standing near you talking with Jesus? I would love to see this: wouldn't you? I am certain that these disciples were stunned and in awe as they witnessed these amazing things. In shock, Peter blurted out, *"Rabbi, it is good for us to be here; and let us make three tabernacles: one for You, one for Moses, and one for Elijah"—because he did not know what to say, for they were greatly afraid."* (Mark 9:5) If you don't know what to say, it is wise not to say anything at all.

Another beautiful picture of our Father God is seen by how He deals with Peter's outburst. The loving and gracious Father God simply appeared in a cloud and overshadowed these awe struck disciples before speaking to Peter. This was the first time the cloud of His glory had appeared for many centuries. Instead of a strong rebuke for Peter, the Lord overshadowed them and spoke something very powerful into their lives.

> *"And a cloud came and overshadowed them; and a voice came out of the cloud, saying, 'This is My beloved Son. Hear Him!' Suddenly, when they had looked around, they saw no one anymore, but only Jesus with themselves."* (Mark 9:7-8)

REVELATION OF GOD'S ATTRIBUTES

As in the earlier manifestations of the glory, we are given powerful revelation about the attributes of God in the person of Yeshua ha Messiach. The first and most powerful of these revelations is a greater understanding of the depth of the Father's love for us. Have you ever wondered about how much the Lord loves you? All you have to do is look at what He did for you through the life, death, and resurrection of Jesus. He loves you enough to let His one and only Son suffer and die on the cross so that you can be restored to fellowship with Him. As you meditate on this, you will get a much deeper understanding of the statement: *"And we have known and believed the love that God has for us. God is love, and he who abides in love abides in God, and God in him."* (1 John 4:16)

This is much more powerful than saying that God has love. He is love! God is love, and He made that ultimately clear when He sent Jesus to make a way for us to come home to the Father! Amen? It is significant that one of those who saw the cloud on the Mountain and heard the voice of God speaking is also the one who is explaining the depth of God's love for us. John is saying that they saw it, experienced it, and know it with certainty – God is love! Study the passage below and reflect on this foundational truth and seek to fully understand the depth of the revelation which John is trying to release to you.

"No one has seen God at any time. If we love one another, God abides in us, and His love has been perfected in us. By this we know that we abide in Him, and He in us, because He has given us of His Spirit. And we have seen and testify that the Father has sent the Son as Savior of the world. Whoever confesses that Jesus is the Son of God, God abides in him, and he in God. And we have known and believed the love that God has for us. God is love, and he who abides in love abides in God, and God in him. (1 John 4:12-16)

In addition to this powerful revelation of His love, we also see the longsuffering and patience of the Lord. He did not chastise Peter for blurting something out when He should have kept quiet. The Father simply explains His relationship with Jesus and asks them to listen to Him. Everything we see in the life and work of Jesus reminds us of the Lord's response to Moses' request to see His glory. *"Then He said, 'I will make all My goodness pass before you, and I will proclaim the name of the Lord before you. I will be gracious to whom I will be gracious, and I will have compassion on whom I will have compassion.'"* (Exodus 33:19) The glory which we see in Jesus is the exact representation of what we are shown about the Father. His goodness is His glory. He chooses to be gracious and compassionate. These are two more awesome and holy attributes of the Lord which we can see when we experience His glory. We know and have confidence in the reality that Jesus is just like the Father.

Jesus said to him, "Have I been with you so long, and yet you have not known Me, Philip? He who has seen Me has seen the Father; so how can you say, 'Show us the Father'?" (John 14:9)

As I was writing this, I was listening to some praise music which gave a quote from the old hymn *"Praise to the Lord, the Almighty"* (Joachim Neander, 1863, Public Domain) *"Ponder anew what the Almighty can do, if with His love He befriend thee."* That is really good advice: Ponder anew! As the old evangelists used to say, "Think about it!" Think about what Almighty God can do for you since He has already befriended all who are in Christ Jesus. Spend a few minutes really thinking about it. Allow the wonderful attributes of God seen in His glory (Yeshua) to sink deeply into your spirit. Volumes could be written on the revelation of the attributes of Father God which we are able to see in Jesus. Make it your lifelong practice to uncover more of His attributes and to soak in the knowledge of what they means to and for you. Begin to let more and more of these attributes manifest in your own life and in your work for the Kingdom of God.

THE GLORY WILL SOON RETURN

"Then the sign of the Son of Man will appear in heaven, and then all the tribes of the earth will mourn, and they will see the Son of Man coming on the clouds of heaven with power and great glory. And He will send His angels with a great sound of a trumpet, and they will gather together His elect from the four winds, from one end of heaven to the other." (Matthew 24:30-31)

The second coming of Yeshua ha Messiach will be even more glorious than the first. When he returns, He will come with both great power and great glory. Many people failed to see His glory during the time He ministered in the flesh. Some of them actually chose not to see it. However, that will not be an option when He returns. For some it will be an occasion of great mourning because they have refused to believe in Him whom they now see as the one true Son of God. For others it will be a time of great rejoicing because their final redemption will arrive and fulfill all His promises. Which group will you be in? Now is a good time to confirm your relationship with the King of kings and Lord of lords. Pray the prayer below to accept Him as King in your heart:

Jesus, I believe in you! I believe that you are the Son of God who died in my place so that my sins could be covered. I believe that you were raised from the dead and ascended into Heaven to sit at the right hand of Father God. I confess my sin and ask your forgiveness. I love you and promise to obey you so that the Father can come in His glory and dwell in my heart! I am now claiming the promise of Romans 10:9-11 (NIV),

"That if you confess with your mouth, "Jesus is Lord," and believe in your heart that God raised him from the dead, you will be saved. For it is with your heart that you believe and are justified, and it is with your mouth that you confess and are saved. As the Scripture says, "Anyone who trusts in him will never be put to shame."

As you pray this prayer aloud, you are making your confession that Jesus is Lord and that God raised Him from the dead. Now you simply accept your salvation by faith and begin to live for Him. Receive by faith the promise in Romans 10:13 (NIV), *"Everyone who calls on the name of the Lord will be saved."* It really is that simple and that easy. Jesus did all the heavy lifting for you. He paid your debt and covered you with His robe of righteousness. Now you have been made ready for His return. Begin now to expect it and look forward to it. This will be the fulfillment of all His promises to you. *"For the Son of Man will come in the glory of His Father with His angels, and then He will reward each according to his works."* (Matthew 16:27)

For some people, this promise does not seem pleasant. They don't want to be rewarded according to their works, because they have not really been obedient to Him. This happens when people do not have a full picture of what He has done for them. When you accept Jesus, you will be rewarded according to His works which have been accounted to you as righteousness. Once again we see the fulfillment of the Lord's word to Moses. His glory is His goodness. His glory in your life is His goodness to you and to all who have made Yeshua their Messiach.

Many people have chosen not to accept Jesus as their Savior because they are not willing to give up what they have in order to receive Him. This often happens because of a great misunderstanding of Him and His goodness (glory) extended to us. We don't give up anything of value. On the contrary we gain everything of eternal value. This is another manifestation of the glory of God.

"So Jesus said to them, 'Assuredly I say to you, that in the regeneration, when the Son of Man sits on the throne of His glory, you who have followed Me will also sit on twelve thrones, judging the twelve tribes of Israel. And everyone who has left houses or brothers or sisters or father or mother or wife or children or lands, for My name's sake, shall receive a hundredfold, and inherit eternal life. But many who are first will be last, and the last first.'" (Matthew 19:28-30)

As you consider these things it may sound a little bit too good to be true. Never forget that the true glory of God is seen in His amazing and awe inspiring goodness. He is concerned about every little detail in your life and He is always present to work His goodness to meet your every need. You can see this in the first miracle of Jesus' ministry. He attended a wedding with His mother and the disciples. The family hosting the wedding made a miscalculation and did not provide an adequate supply of wine for the celebration. Jesus cared enough about this little detail to work a miracle to prevent them from being embarrassed.

Notice the summary of this miracle as reported in John 2:11, *"This beginning of signs Jesus did in Cana of Galilee, and manifested His glory; and His disciples believed in Him."* By this miracle His glory was manifested, because the goodness of God was revealed. Seeing this, the disciples experienced an increase in their faith. The glory of God always brings these kinds of results. Don't fear the glory of God! Embrace it!

The more you see and experience the glory of God the more amazing and wonderful it appears. The glory (manifest presence) of God was so strong in Jesus that he had power over our greatest enemy – death. Jesus interrupted every funeral He attended. He brought the son of a widow in the village of Nain back to life during the procession to his burial place. He raised the dead daughter of a Synagogue leader named Jairus. Jesus raised Lazarus, the brother of Martha and Mary, back from the dead after he had been dead and buried for four days. Immediately following this miracle, Jesus connected resurrection power and authority to the glory of God. *"Jesus said to her* (Martha), *"Did I not say to you that if you would believe you would see the glory of God?"* (John 11:40) Imagine what you will see if you believe in Jesus. You will see even greater things than these as the glory of God is revealed more and more.

> *"But if the ministry of death, written and engraved on stones, was glorious, so that the children of Israel could not look steadily at the face of Moses because of the glory of his countenance, which glory was passing away, how will the ministry of the Spirit not be more glorious?"* 2 Corinthians 3:7-8

BENEFITS OF THE GLORY IN YESHUA

There are certain things you can begin to expect as you experience the glory of God in Jesus. *"For if the ministry of condemnation had glory, the ministry of righteousness exceeds much more in glory. For even what was made glorious had no glory in this respect, because of the glory that excels. For if what is passing away was glorious, what remains is much more glorious."* (2 Corinthians 3:9-11) I have listed a few of the things which the glory in Jesus brings. As you study the list below, begin to add to it what the Lord reveals to you. I don't expect to exhaust this list during my lifetime. Perhaps we will still be adding to it during all eternity.

THE GLORY IN JESUS BRINGS:

> *"And now, O Father, glorify Me together with Yourself, with the glory which I had with You before the world was."* (John 17:5)

1. His glory brings perfect redemption, a new life, and eternal life.

"Therefore we were buried with Him through baptism into death, that just as Christ was raised from the dead by the glory of the Father, even so we also should walk in newness of life." (Romans 6:4)

2. A new call to obedience is given as we experience His glory.

"Jesus answered and said to him, "If anyone loves Me, he will keep My word; and My Father will love him, and We will come to him and make Our home with him." (John 14:23)

3. We are given a huge increase in our ability to experience His love.

"And the glory which You gave Me I have given them, that they may be one just as We are one: I in them, and You in Me; that they may be made perfect in one, and that the world may know that You have sent Me, and have loved them as You have loved Me." (John 17:22-23)

a. Love increases our capacity for gifts.
b. Love increases our capacity for authority.
c. Love increases our capacity to minister with God's power.
d. Love increases our capacity for blessing and favor.

4. His weighty presence imparts glory to you.

"...and when the Chief Shepherd appears, you will receive the crown of glory that does not fade away." (1 Peter 5:4)

a. Intimacy with Jesus glows on you because of His impartation of glory.

"For it is the God who commanded light to shine out of darkness, who has shone in our hearts to give the light of the knowledge of the glory of God in the face of Jesus Christ." (2 Corinthians 4:6)

b. Remember that it is a fading glory as with Moses.
c. To retain it, you must stay in His presence.

5. The Living Word of God dwells in you.

"And the Word became flesh and dwelt among us, and we beheld His glory, the glory as of the only begotten of the Father, full of grace and truth." (John 1:14)

6. It enables you to see the truth of who Jesus is and what that means for you.

"But even if our gospel is veiled, it is veiled to those who are perishing, whose minds the god of this age has blinded, who do not believe, lest the light of the gospel of the glory of Christ, who is the image of God, should shine on them." (2 Corinthians 4:3-4)

7. The judge and your savior are the same person: Yeshua ha Messiach!

"When the Son of Man comes in His glory, and all the holy angels with Him, then He will sit on the throne of His glory. All the nations will be gathered before Him, and He will separate them one from another, as a shepherd divides his sheep from the goats." (Matthew 25:31-32)

8. All of these things were done for you and bring glory to God.

"What if God, wanting to show His wrath and to make His power known, endured with much longsuffering the vessels of wrath prepared for destruction, and that He might make known the riches of His glory on the vessels of mercy, which He had prepared beforehand for glory, even us whom He called, not of the Jews only, but also of the Gentiles?" (Romans 9:22-24)

It is important to understand what all of this means for you. I encourage you to begin a lifelong study so that your understanding will constantly increase. Do this so that the knowledge of the fullness of Christ will bring more grace and glory into your life and ministry. The passage below is a little lengthy, but reveals some very powerful truths about the glory of God as revealed in Jesus Christ. I encourage you to study it carefully as you open your heart to be filled with the glory of God and all the fullness of Jesus Christ's work in you.

"For you have not come to the mountain that may be touched and that burned with fire, and to blackness and darkness and tempest, and the sound of a trumpet and the voice of words, so that those who heard it begged that the word should not be spoken to them anymore. (For they could not endure what was commanded: "And if so much as a beast touches the mountain, it shall be stoned or shot with an arrow." And so terrifying was the sight that Moses said, "I am exceedingly afraid and trembling.") But you have come to Mount Zion and to the city of the living God, the heavenly Jerusalem, to an innumerable company of angels, to the general assembly and church of the firstborn who are registered in heaven, to God the Judge of all, to the spirits of just men made

perfect, to Jesus the Mediator of the new covenant, and to the blood of sprinkling that speaks better things than that of Abel." (Hebrews 12:18-24)

THE PRAYER OF JESUS FOR YOU

"*Father, I desire that they also whom You gave Me may be with Me where I am, that they may behold My glory which You have given Me; for You loved Me before the foundation of the world. O righteous Father! The world has not known You, but I have known You; and these have known that You sent Me. And I have declared to them Your name, and will declare it, that the love with which You loved Me may be in them, and I in them.*" (John 17:24-26)

THE PRAYER OF PAUL FOR YOU

"*For this reason I bow my knees to the Father of our Lord Jesus Christ, from whom the whole family in heaven and earth is named, that He would grant you, according to the riches of His glory, to be strengthened with might through His Spirit in the inner man, that Christ may dwell in your hearts through faith; that you, being rooted and grounded in love, may be able to comprehend with all the saints what is the width and length and depth and height—to know the love of Christ which passes knowledge; that you may be filled with all the fullness of God.*" (Ephesians 3:14-19)

SELAH QUESTIONS

1. Who is the King of Glory?

2. What is the relationship between Jesus and the glory of God?

3. In what ways have you seen the glory of God in your own life and ministry?

4. What benefits does the glory in Jesus bring to you?

5. How can you show the glory of God to others?

6. Make a list of the things Jesus prayed for you so that you will be enabled to experience His glory!

CHAPTER 8

LEVEL 7: THE SPIRIT OF GLORY IN US

—◦◦◦—

"When the Day of Pentecost had fully come, they were all with one accord in one place. And suddenly there came a sound from heaven, as of a rushing mighty wind, and it filled the whole house where they were sitting. Then there appeared to them divided tongues, as of fire, and one sat upon each of them. And they were all filled with the Holy Spirit and began to speak with other tongues, as the Spirit gave them utterance." (Acts 2:1-4)

God's seventh step in bringing His glory down to us began on the Day of Pentecost. In this seventh level of His glory, we experience the Lord moving His weighty presence from the outside of His people to the inside. On that day, the indwelling presence of the Holy Spirit came to everyone present in the Upper Room. They were all *"filled with the Holy Spirit."* Each of these 120 disciples experienced the fulfillment of the promise given by John the Baptist: *"I indeed baptize you with water unto repentance, but He who is coming after me is mightier than I, whose sandals I am not worthy to carry. He will baptize you with the Holy Spirit and fire."* (Matthew 3:11) They received both parts of this promise on the same day: 1) the baptism of the Holy Spirit, and 2) the baptism of Fire.

As with previous manifestations of God's glory, the outpouring of the Holy Spirit on the Day of Pentecost gives us a wealth of revelation knowledge about the Lord's precious and powerful attributes. Once again we experience Father God as a promise keeper. He keeps His Word and we can always count on Him regardless of what our circumstances may be saying to us at the moment. Notice the similarity of the manifestation of the glory on the day of Pentecost with the glory of the Lord which appeared when the Temple was dedicated.

"When Solomon had finished praying, fire came down from heaven and consumed the burnt offering and the sacrifices; and the glory of the Lord filled the temple." (2 Chronicles 7:1)

One of the Lord's powerful attributes is consistency and reliability. We can count on Him to always be the same. He is the same yesterday, today and forever (Hebrews 13:8). He is the giver of good things and that will not change. Remember what James said, *"Every good gift and every perfect gift is from above, and comes down from the Father of lights, with whom there is no variation or shadow of turning."* (James 1:17) The Lord is the giver of good and perfect gifts and the Holy Spirit is one of those awesome and wonderful gifts from the Father. Jesus said it this way, *"If you then, being evil, know how to give good gifts to your children, how much more will your heavenly Father give the Holy Spirit to those who ask Him!"* (Luke 11:13) Once again, you can see His glory in His goodness. The Lord is good! He is good all the time! He doesn't even make a shadow of turning away from us. He is consistent and reliable in His goodness toward us. It is a great joy to join with the saints of all the periods of history and proclaim: *"For He is good, for His mercy endures forever."* (2 Chronicles 7:3b) These two attributes (goodness and consistency) always go hand in hand. Therefore, we can with all confidence place our faith, hope, and future in His hands. The Holy Spirit is the key to understanding so much of what Father God intends for His children as we are welcomed into His eternal kingdom even while still living on the Earth.

> *"So Jesus answered and said, 'Assuredly, I say to you, there is no one who has left house or brothers or sisters or father or mother or wife or children or lands, for My sake and the gospel's, who shall not receive a hundredfold now in this time—houses and brothers and sisters and mothers and children and lands, with persecutions—and in the age to come, eternal life.'"* (Mark 10:29-30)

In this manifestation of His glory, we also see that the Lord is our provider. He is the source for all we need and He is faithful to meet all our needs. This is true whether we are speaking of the spirit, the soul, or the body. The Lord provides for all these areas of our needs. The Holy Spirit comes to provide for the soul when He appears as the comforter, counselor, and advisor. He also provides for our bodies through miracles, healings, signs and wonders. *"God also bearing witness both with signs and wonders, with various miracles, and gifts of the Holy Spirit, according to His own will?"* (Hebrews 2:4) In addition to all of these things, He continues to minister to our spirits through the twin processes of regeneration and renewal.

> *"But when the kindness and the love of God our Savior toward man appeared, not by works of righteousness which we have done, but according to His mercy He saved us, through the washing of regeneration and renewing of the Holy Spirit, whom He poured out on us abundantly through Jesus Christ our Savior, that having been justified by His grace we should become heirs according to the hope of eternal life."* (Titus 3:4-7)

When the Holy Spirit manifests as the Spirit of truth, He is the source of a massive amount of revelation knowledge. This promise of the Lord is only for believers. It is given as an impartation directly from the Lord. *"And when He had said this, He breathed on them, and said to them, "Receive the Holy Spirit."* (John 20:22) He is still breathing on His disciples, and imparting the Holy Spirit to provide all they need to accomplish their God given destiny for the Kingdom.

The world has never been able to really grasp spiritual truth or understand the realm of the Spirit, because it does not have the Spirit of truth. *"We are of God. He who knows God hears us; he who is not of God does not hear us. By this we know the spirit of truth and the spirit of error."* (1 John 4:6) You can only receive these powerful truths when the Holy Spirit dwells in you. Do you know Him? If you don't know Him this is a good time to pray and ask the Lord to dwell in you. Remember that the Lord is faithful to give the Holy Spirit to those who ask. Place a claim on the promise of Jesus given in the fourteenth chapter of John:

"If you love Me, keep My commandments. And I will pray the Father, and He will give you another Helper, that He may abide with you forever—the Spirit of truth, whom the world cannot receive, because it neither sees Him nor knows Him; but you know Him, for He dwells with you and will be in you. I will not leave you orphans; I will come to you." (John 14:15-18)

The Spirit of truth accomplishes this work in several ways. First, He is your daily companion, guide, and counselor. He provides what you need both now and in the future. In times of crisis, He is presence within you to tell you what to say and what to do. Meditate on the passage below and reflect on the times the Holy Spirit has already done this for you. Then begin to build up your faith that He will continue to do this in the future.

"Now when they bring you to the synagogues and magistrates and authorities, do not worry about how or what you should answer, or what you should say. For the Holy Spirit will teach you in that very hour what you ought to say." (Luke 12:11-12)

As you begin to understand more and more of what the Lord has provided for you through the work of the Holy Spirit, you will see that He is the key to unlock so many of the blessings Father God has provided for you. The Bible gives many different images to help you understand the Holy Spirit and the depth and breadth of His work in you. Take a few moments to consider how He is the Key to unlocking your inheritance right now. Below, I suggest several ways in which The Holy Spirit is the key, and I encourage you to seek revelation and understanding from the Lord to expand on these.

THE HOLY SPIRIT AS THE KEY

1. THE KEY TO THE ADVENT OF CHRIST

"Now the birth of Jesus Christ was as follows: After His mother Mary was betrothed to Joseph, before they came together, she was found with child of the Holy Spirit." (Matthew 1:18)

More than in any other part of the Scriptures, we see the goodness of God when He sent His one and only Son to suffer and die on the cross to make a way for us to be restored to His loving family. This amazing and powerful work through the Lord Jesus was also from beginning to end a work of the Holy Spirit. It was the Holy Spirit who planted the divine seed into Mary's womb. In the same way, the Holy Spirit plants the seed of faith in each of our hearts. When we experience the new birth, it is the Holy Spirit who makes it real and effective in our own hearts.

144

"However, when He, the Spirit of truth, has come, He will guide you into all truth; for He will not speak on His own authority, but whatever He hears He will speak; and He will tell you things to come. He will glorify Me, for He will take of what is Mine and declare it to you." (John 16:13-14)

Just as the Holy Spirit was the agent by which the divine seed was brought into the world, He is also the agent to plant the spiritual reality of Christ in each of us. In this season of the Lord, He is the primary source for divine spiritual truth for each of us. Someone may ask, "But, what about the scriptures? Aren't the scriptures the primary source of truth for us?" The answer is, "Yes and No!" Yes the Bible is our primary source. However, the scriptures are only truly understood as they are spiritually discerned. The "No" answer is our acknowledgement that we can only grasp Biblical truth if the Holy Spirit reveals it to us.

"We have not received the spirit of the world but the Spirit who is from God, that we may understand what God has freely given us. This is what we speak, not in words taught us by human wisdom but in words taught by the Spirit, expressing spiritual truths in spiritual words. The man without the Spirit does not accept the things that come from the Spirit of God, for they are foolishness to him, and he cannot understand them, because they are spiritually discerned." (1 Corinthians 2:12-14, NIV)

2. THE KEY TO THE RESURRECTION OF CHRIST

"and who through the Spirit of holiness was declared with power to be the Son of God by his resurrection from the dead: Jesus Christ our Lord." (Romans 1:4, NIV)

As I mentioned above, the saving work of Jesus Christ is also from start to finish a work of the Holy Spirit. At the start:

145

"When He had been baptized, Jesus came up immediately from the water; and behold, the heavens were opened to Him, and He saw the Spirit of God descending like a dove and alighting upon Him." (Matthew 3:16) The Holy Spirit filled Him and remained with Him throughout His earthly ministry. The passage above from the book of Romans is a very strong reminder that the power for the resurrection of Jesus manifested through a declaration made by the Holy Spirit. The Holy Spirit planted the seed and raised it from the dead so that Yeshua ha Messiach could be the first-fruits of all those who will be raised to eternal life. As you meditate on the passage below, think about how important this is to your own resurrection to eternal life:

"It is the Spirit who gives life; the flesh profits nothing. The words that I speak to you are spirit, and they are life." (John 6:63)

From the beginning of His ministry, Jesus clearly taught that the source of life is the Holy Spirit. Jesus still speaks these Spirit filled and Spirit empowered words of life, and the Holy Spirit brings them into manifestation. As you meditate on these Biblical truths, consider how the Holy Spirit is doing this work in your life. When you speak and declare the spirit filled words of life given by the Lord Jesus, the Holy Spirit adds the power of God to the message and releases the Life (Zoe) of God into the hearts and minds of the lost. It is an amazing and wonderful thing that the Lord allows us to participate in this awesome work.

3. THE KEY TO VICTORY OVER THE WORLD

"But he, being full of the Holy Spirit, gazed into heaven and saw the glory of God, and Jesus standing at the right hand of God, and said, "Look! I see the heavens opened and the Son of Man standing at the right hand of God!" (Acts 7:55-56)

146

Stephen was empowered to face a painful death at the hands of an angry mob because he was "full of the Holy Spirit." In the hour of his greatest need, the Holy Spirit opened his eyes to see into heaven. As Stephen saw the glory of God and Jesus standing at His right hand, he knew that everything he had believed and taught was absolutely true. He courageously testified to what the Holy Spirit had shown him even though it enraged the mob to assault him further. Then something really amazing happened. The mind of Christ manifested in his last moments on Earth. Just as Jesus had done on the cross, he prayed for the forgiveness of those who were murdering him. All of this came as a powerful work of the Holy Spirit.

4. THE KEY TO UNDERSTANDING THE GOSPEL

"But the Helper, the Holy Spirit, whom the Father will send in My name, He will teach you all things, and bring to your remembrance all things that I said to you." (John 14:26)

One of the realities of the human condition is that memories fade with time. It would have been easy for the message of the gospel to be exaggerated or for parts to be forgotten and left out as the years went by. However, the Lord made sure this would not happen. He gave the Holy Spirit to help those early disciples and disciples today to know and teach the truth about the gospel of the Kingdom of God. The Holy Spirit gave them remembrance of the things Jesus said so they could write them down and make them available to you and me today. The Holy Spirit has also been given to you and will guide you to stay on the path of truth. As you study and teach the Word of God, seek the help of the Holy Spirit to make sure that what you are saying and doing are based on the truth of God.

5. THE KEY TO BEING THE TEMPLE

"Or do you not know that your body is the temple of the Holy Spirit who is in you, whom you have from God, and you are not your own?" (1 Corinthians 6:19)

Over the years I have listened to many teachings about the temple of God in those who love and obey Jesus. However, I have not heard many messages which speak of the *"temple of the Holy Spirit who is in you."* Even this plan of God to make you His Temple is a work of the Holy Spirit. If you want to fully experience this wonderful gift from God, you need to let Him clean and consecrate the place of His Holy Presence. This process of cleansing your heart to make it a suitable habitation for the Lord is also a work of the Holy Spirit. Therefore, the Holy Spirit is the key to having the glory of God abiding in and working through you.

6. THE KEY TO OUR FRUITFULNESS

"But the fruit of the Spirit is love, joy, peace, longsuffering, kindness, goodness, faithfulness, gentleness, self-control. Against such there is no law." (Galatians 5:22)

Have you considered the fact that the very best parts of who you are and what you do with your life are actually gifts from God through the Holy Spirit? When the Holy Spirit takes up residence in His Temple (in your heart), His attributes are imparted to you. You begin to do things for others which He is doing in your life. You begin to speak what He speaks. You begin to behave toward others as He behaves toward you. There is no law against these things, because the purpose of the Torah is to teach you to understand and begin to manifest the attributes of God.

Remember that the glory of God is seen in His goodness. *"...for the fruit of the Spirit is in all goodness, righteousness, and truth,*" (Ephesians 5:9) As the Lord puts His glory into your heart you begin to produce similar fruit in your ministry for others. When this begins to manifest, people will see the glory of God in the goodness manifested in your life and work. Failing to show these attributes freely given to you is a serious breach of faith with God and the Holy Spirit. When these things are not visible to others, they will miss seeing God's glory, and then they will likely do less to acknowledge and praise Him. He will not receive the glory which is due to Him from His work in and through us.

7. THE KEY TO SPIRITUAL GIFTING

"There are diversities of gifts, but the same Spirit. There are differences of ministries, but the same Lord. And there are diversities of activities, but it is the same God who works all in all. But the manifestation of the Spirit is given to each one for the profit of all: for to one is given the word of wisdom through the Spirit, to another the word of knowledge through the same Spirit, to another faith by the same Spirit, to another gifts of healings by the same Spirit, to another the working of miracles, to another prophecy, to another discerning of spirits, to another different kinds of tongues, to another the interpretation of tongues. But one and the same Spirit works all these things, distributing to each one individually as He wills." (1 Corinthians 12:4-11)

The world tends to honor people with gifts rather than the giver of the gifts. People like to think that their talents, abilities, and accomplishments bring glory to themselves. However, Spirit-led people know that all these things are gifts from God and when they are enabled to manifest His attributes all of the glory belongs to Him. Every good and perfect gift comes from above and all of the glory needs to be given to the Father above.

Gifts and talents fade quickly as time takes its toll on the human body, but the power of God released in His gifts never fades or diminishes. We see a man like Moses who got his start at the age of eighty. Caleb finally got his chance to deal with the giants at the ripe young age of eighty-five. What can the Lord do through you right now if you will allow the gifts of the Spirit to work in your life and ministry? Think about it!

8. THE KEY TO SECURING YOUR INHERITANCE

"In Him also we have obtained an inheritance, being predestined according to the purpose of Him who works all things according to the counsel of His will, that we who first trusted in Christ should be to the praise of His glory. (Ephesians 1:11-12)

Most, if not all, people like the idea of receiving an inheritance. Some people have waited for most of their lives to receive something from a wealthy relative. But you don't have to wait. Your inheritance is available to you right now! You have an inheritance from the Father who owns everything. It is a deception of the enemy that you have to wait until you die to receive it. You receive it because Jesus died and left it to you. He promised that it was for this present life as well as for eternity. Receive it now! The Holy Spirit is your guarantee for your inheritance, and He has access to all of it right now. It is a sealed promise! Take it and use it for the work of the Kingdom of God in the world right now.

"In Him you also trusted, after you heard the word of truth, the gospel of your salvation; in whom also, having believed, you were sealed with the Holy Spirit of promise, who is the guarantee of our inheritance until the redemption of the purchased possession, to the praise of His glory." (Ephesians 1:13-14)

150

9. THE KEY TO EXPERIENCING THE GLORY

"But if the ministry of death, written and engraved on stones, was glorious, so that the children of Israel could not look steadily at the face of Moses because of the glory of his countenance, which glory was passing away, how will the ministry of the Spirit not be more glorious?" (2 Corinthians 3:7-8)

Can you imagine that? The ministry of the Spirit is much more glorious through you than what Moses experienced on Mount Sinai. Wow! That is an amazing and wonderful thought. Are you ready to receive it? Study the passage below and ask the Holy Spirit to give you deep revelation knowledge about the fullness of this promise. Many people only accept the first part of the promise: to receive comfort when they are reproached. But the promise is so much greater than that. Think about it! The Spirit of glory and of God rests on you! He is on you and in you! He works through you to bring more glory to God. All of this is available to you! Become a good host for the Spirit of glory and watch what God can do through your life and ministry! This is awesome!

"If you are reproached for the name of Christ, blessed are you, for the Spirit of glory and of God rests upon you. On their part He is blasphemed, but on your part He is glorified." (1 Peter 4:14)

10. THE KEY TO THE ONE NEW MAN CHURCH

"For through Him we both have access by one Spirit to the Father." (Ephesians 2:18)

This concept is so huge that it would take volumes to understand and teach the fullness of what the Spirit is doing to bring us together in the Father. The key to unifying all things is the

Holy Spirit. He is the active agent of God to make it manifest through us. Unfortunately, many believers resist this work of the Holy Spirit. They are not willing to be changed in order to be made fit for this new thing from the Lord. They want things to remain the same so they can somehow feel sufficient and somewhat superior in the way they are now. If you resist the Holy Spirit, you may miss the greatest manifestation of the glory the world has ever seen. Study the passage below and ask again for revelation knowledge from the Holy Spirit.

> *"For He Himself is our peace, who has made both one, and has broken down the middle wall of separation, having abolished in His flesh the enmity, that is, the law of commandments contained in ordinances, so as to create in Himself one new man from the two, thus making peace, and that He might reconcile them both to God in one body through the cross, thereby putting to death the enmity. And He came and preached peace to you who were afar off and to those who were near."* (Ephesians 2:14-17)

11. THE KEY TO PROPHETIC UTTERANCE

> *"For David himself said by the Holy Spirit: 'The Lord said to my Lord, Sit at My right hand, till I make Your enemies Your footstool.'"* (Mark 12:36)

From the days of the Old Testament prophets until this day, all prophetic gifting is through the Holy Spirit. The Bible makes this clear in the passage above. David spoke through the Holy Spirit. In the same way, we are told that the father of John the Baptist prophesied through the work of the Holy Spirit. *"Now his father Zacharias was filled with the Holy Spirit, and prophesied, saying:"* (Luke 1:67)

Paul made it clear that prophetic gifting is still available for Spirit-led people today. *"Pursue love, and desire spiritual gifts, but especially that you may prophesy."* (1 Corinthians 14:1) In these troubled times, this gift is greatly needed by the Body of Christ. *"But everyone who prophesies speaks to men for their strengthening, encouragement and comfort."* (1 Corinthians 14:3, NIV) Do you know people who need to be strengthened, encouraged, and comforted? Who is the promise for? It is for all believers! Look again at what Paul said in 1 Corinthians 14:31, *"For you can all prophesy one by one, that all may learn and all may be encouraged."* The Lord is still providing this ministry through the prophetic gifting released by the Holy Spirit. Receive it and minister it!

12. THE KEY TO MORE EFFECTIVE PRAYER

"But you, beloved, building yourselves up on your most holy faith, praying in the Holy Spirit, keep yourselves in the love of God, looking for the mercy of our Lord Jesus Christ unto eternal life." (Jude 1:20-21)

You don't have to wait for someone else to build you up with a prophetic word. You have the Holy Spirit and using your prayer language you can release this in your own spirit. You can build up your most holy faith. You can keep yourself in the love of God. You can receive His mercy to meet every need. Just take it all to the Lord in prayer. Pray in the Holy Spirit! Use your prayer language to release these things for you, your family, your church, and the lost.

13. THE KEY TO PRAYERS OF REPENTANCE

"And I will pour on the house of David and on the inhabitants of Jerusalem the Spirit of grace and supplication; then they will look on Me whom they pierced. Yes, they will mourn for Him as one mourns for his only son, and grieve for Him as one grieves for a firstborn." (Zechariah 12:10a)

153

When the Word became flesh and ministered on the earth, many people rejected Him and missed the opportunity of a lifetime. They did not receive the Holy Spirit, and could not discern who He was and what He was doing. They were offended by Him and by the message He preached. But it didn't have to be that way! They could have asked, and would have been given the Holy Spirit to help them understand, repent and return to the Father. This doesn't have to happen to you. Father God still gives the Spirit of grace and supplication to His people in order to draw them back into the family. This gift is available to you and me today.

Have you missed something the Lord has tried to reveal to you? Have you denied Him before others? Have you gone through periods of doubt and disobedience? Have you rebelled against the King of Glory? Don't despair! The Lord has provided a way back for you. This is so important that Father God revealed it before the birth of Christ. Read the passage above from Zechariah chapter twelve again and meditate on what the Spirit is revealing to you. I pray that you will choose to receive the Spirit of grace and supplication and let Him bring you back to the Father!

DON'T LOSE THIS PRECIOUS GIFT!

"And do not grieve the Holy Spirit of God, by whom you were sealed for the day of redemption." (Ephesians 4:30)

There is something so special and unique about the Holy Spirit that the Lord gave a separate rule about our relationship with Him. Many things will be forgiven, but blasphemy against the Holy Spirit will not be forgiven in this life or the next. We must be very careful in this area. Do not grieve or blaspheme the Holy Spirit! Your eternal life depends on it!

"'Assuredly, I say to you, all sins will be forgiven the sons of men, and whatever blasphemies they may utter; but he

who blasphemes against the Holy Spirit never has forgiveness, but is subject to eternal condemnation'—because they said, 'He has an unclean spirit.'" (Mark 3:28-30)

If you are concerned about this, I am certain that you have not done it. When you lose the Holy Spirit, your conscience will be seared, and you will no longer be able to be concerned or repentant about it. The message here is that you must not do it. Jesus taught clearly that this sin is about attributing the work of the Holy Spirit to the devil and vice versa. Study the passage above and the accounts of this incident in the other gospels. Understand what Jesus is teaching about this sin and then decide for yourself. Always remember the consequences of insulting the Spirit of grace.

"Of how much worse punishment, do you suppose, will he be thought worthy who has trampled the Son of God underfoot, counted the blood of the covenant by which he was sanctified a common thing, and insulted the Spirit of grace?" (Hebrews 10:29)

PRAYER

"For this reason I kneel before the Father, from whom his whole family in heaven and on earth derives its name. I pray that out of his glorious riches he may strengthen you with power through his Spirit in your inner being, so that Christ may dwell in your hearts through faith. And I pray that you, being rooted and established in love, may have power, together with all the saints, to grasp how wide and long and high and deep is the love of Christ, and to know this love that surpasses knowledge—that you may be filled to the measure of all the fullness of God." (Ephesians 3:14-19, NIV)

SELAH QUESTIONS

1. Have you been baptized in the Holy Spirit and fire? If so, how has that manifested in your life and work?

2. How is the glory of God made manifest by the Holy Spirit?

3. What attributes of God are made manifest in the work of the Holy Spirit?

4. Name and explain four of the key things which the Lord does through the Holy Spirit.

5. What is the unpardonable sin? How can you avoid it?

CHAPTER 9

THE BRIDGE

"Now the Lord is the Spirit; and where the Spirit of the Lord is, there is liberty. But we all, with unveiled face, beholding as in a mirror the glory of the Lord, are being transformed into the same image from glory to glory, just as by the Spirit of the Lord." (2 Corinthians 3:17-18)

In the same way that the glory of the Lord comes down in seven distinct manifestations, we are lifted back up and transformed into his image in seven distinct works of the Holy Spirit. As you consider this, remember the prophetic significance of the number seven. In addition to being an exact number it also refers to completeness or fullness. In any one of these seven levels, you may see additional levels beyond the one you are currently experiencing. The number seven may also indicate that more levels will be revealed later. You may be made aware of some of these while you meditate on those listed below. In other words, do not try to limit God and His ability to give you deeper and deeper revelations of how He works to accomplish His glorious purpose.

One powerful example of this is seen in the fourth chapter of the book of Acts. Long after the outpouring on the day of Pentecost, the early disciples received a second experience of being filled with the Holy Spirit. This event is documented in the passage below. Within the seventh level of the manifestation of the glory of God a second level is revealed to those who prayed for boldness to proclaim the gospel during a time of intense persecution. This manifestation came in response to their sincere prayers for empowerment from the Lord. This serves as a clear example of how the Lord can put levels within each level and add a level as He wills. It is all in accordance with His will and His purposes in our lives.

> *"And when they had prayed, the place where they were assembled together was shaken; and they were all filled with the Holy Spirit, and they spoke the word of God with boldness. Now the multitude of those who believed were of one heart and one soul; neither did anyone say that any of the things he possessed was his own, but they had all things in common. And with great power the apostles gave witness to the resurrection of the Lord Jesus. And great grace was upon them all. Nor was there anyone among them who lacked; for all who were possessors of lands or houses sold them, and brought the proceeds of the things that were sold, and laid them at the apostles' feet; and they distributed to each as anyone had need."*
> (Acts 4:31-35)

As believers in Jesus Christ, we have all been given a great commission by the Lord. He said, *"Go therefore and make disciples of all the nations, baptizing them in the name of the Father and of the Son and of the Holy Spirit,"* (Matthew 28:19) Attempting to accomplish the goals of this commissioning is a very huge undertaking. Then as now, the world we have been sent to evangelize is hostile to the message of the Gospel. In spite of this fact, we have been commanded to make disciples of all these hostile nations. How can we possibly do this? Our only hope is to be filled with the Holy Spirit so that we can be guided and empowered by Father God through Him.

As I considered this grand and glorious undertaking, the Lord revealed something else to me about the seven levels of glory. In the same way that He came down in seven stages (seven levels), He plans to lift us up through seven levels so that we can be restored to the image He intended in the creation. We are being taken from glory to glory into this image. Again, think about the prophetic meaning of the number seven. You may experience additional levels or other levels within a particular level. The listing of these seven levels is not meant to limit what the Lord is doing but to give a framework for understanding more about how the Lord is lifting you up. The seven levels revealed to me are as follow:

1. The Indwelling Level of Glory
2. The Empowerment level of His Glory
3. The Gifting (spiritual gifts) level of His Glory
4. The Joy Level of Glory
5. The Shalom Level of Glory
6. The Intimacy Level of Glory
7. The Unity Level of Glory

The revelation that I received from the Holy Spirit is that these are progressive and generally follow this order in each of our lives. However, God is still God and He can do it any way He chooses. You may have experienced some of these levels simultaneously and find it difficult to separate or distinguish them. That's okay! Ask the Holy Spirit to reveal what you need to know and what you need to do as an obedient disciple. You may have experienced additional levels. That's good. We must let the Lord decide how each of us will experience His glory. Just as spiritual gifts are given according to the will of God, we experience the glory the same way – in accordance with His will.

CHAPTER 10

LEVEL 1: THE INDWELLING GLORY

―⌇⌇⌇―

"Jesus answered and said to him, "If anyone loves Me, he will keep My word; and My Father will love him, and We will come to him and make Our home with him." (John 14:23)

The first thing I want you to see is that this level of glory is directly tied to and follows on from what you studied in Chapter Eight, "The Spirit of Glory in Us." Our beginning point for encountering the glory of God is the infilling of the Holy Spirit. We enter into our experience of these things at that seventh level. Then it becomes for us the first level in our being lifted up from glory to glory into the same image. This level may also be described as "being born again." When the Holy Spirit indwells us, He gives a new form of life to our mortal bodies. Even though these bodies may perish, we will never die. Revelation 20:6, *"Blessed and holy is he who has part in the first resurrection. Over such the second death has no power, but they shall be priests of God and of Christ, and shall reign with Him a thousand years."* After we partake of the resurrection of Jesus Christ, the second death no longer has any power over us. Compare this with the passage below

160

and let these truths merge together and sink deeply into your spirit and soul.

> *"But if the Spirit of Him who raised Jesus from the dead dwells in you, He who raised Christ from the dead will also give life to your mortal bodies through His Spirit who dwells in you."* (Romans 8:11)

Since the primary definition of the word "glory" is the manifest (weighty) presence of the Lord, every word about His indwelling presence is a word about the glory. The Father does this in direct answer to a powerful prayer by our Lord Jesus. Before He died, He prayed for this and many other things for His followers. It is important for you to understand that He was also praying this for you. Let that thought sink into your spirit and strengthen you. Consider how all of this fits together in Jesus' prayer in the passage below!

> *"I do not pray for these alone, but also for those who will believe in Me through their word; that they all may be one, as You, Father, are in Me, and I in You; that they also may be one in Us, that the world may believe that You sent Me. And the glory which You gave Me I have given them, that they may be one just as We are one: I in them, and You in Me; that they may be made perfect in one, and that the world may know that You have sent Me, and have loved them as You have loved Me."* (John 17:20-23)

All of the things which Jesus prayed and decreed in John chapters fourteen through seventeen are for you. Don't buy into some manmade doctrine which says it was only for the twelve. If that was true, Judas would have received the same as the others. You must go back to the truth of the Word and let go of these manmade notions which limit your understanding of what the Lord can and will do both for you and through you. Place a claim on every promise and prayer given by Yeshua ha Messiach. Don't let the enemy steal what the Lord has given you as an inheritance. Claim your inheritance as explained in the passage below:

> *"If you love Me, keep My commandments. And I will pray the Father, and He will give you another Helper, that He may abide with you forever—the Spirit of truth, whom the world cannot receive, because it neither sees Him nor knows Him; but you know Him, for He dwells with you and will be in you. I will not leave you orphans; I will come to you."* (John 14:15-18)

Hallelujah! We have not been left as orphans. We have an inheritance! We have a living Father God. We have a living Lord, Yeshua ha Messiach! Both the Father and the Son have made a decision and decreed it as absolute truth. If you love Jesus and obey His commands, the Father loves you and comes to dwell in you. He comes in the form of that weighty presence of His Holy Spirit. When this happens, you will know that the Lord has released His glory to you. What kind of glory has been given to you? This is another amazing and awesome thought. You have received the same glory that Father God gave to Jesus. Read the next passage aloud several times: *"The same glory you gave me, I gave them, so they'll be as unified and together as we are"* (John 17:22, TMSG)

Why would Father God do this? Jesus makes His purpose clear. He wants to bring the world into unity. By the way, that is the seventh level of glory for us. I am asking you to really listen carefully to the fullness of what Jesus said in the following passage. Don't let a religious spirit and the manmade doctrines it gives limit these promises for you! Don't allow the enemy to steal your destiny and rob you of the gifts of God provided for you in Jesus through the work of the Holy Spirit. Claim the promises of Jesus and hold on to everything the Lord releases to you through the indwelling Holy Spirit.

"I have given them the glory that you gave me, that they may be one as we are one: I in them and you in me. May they be brought to complete unity to let the world know that you sent me and have loved them even as you have loved me." (John 17:22-23, NIV)

This is such an amazing prayer! Jesus is asking Father God to give you the same things given to Him. He asks the Father to love you and me with the same love He has for His only begotten Son, Jesus. He is asking for you to be united with the Father in the same way He is united with Him. Jesus is the mediator and stands in His place seeking to unite us as He has prayed. Try to imagine the power of this. Jesus has given you the same glory which was given to Him, and you can experience this by having the Holy Spirit dwell in you. This literally changes you from being of the flesh to being a person of the Spirit.

"But you are not in the flesh but in the Spirit, if indeed the Spirit of God dwells in you. Now if anyone does not have the Spirit of Christ, he is not His." (Romans 8:9)

Paul had a very firm grasp on the significance of this work of the Holy Spirit. He taught it over and over to people from the various communities where He was sent to minister. Jesus had prophesied the destruction of the physical Temple in Jerusalem. When the disciples were in awe of the magnificent buildings of the Temple complex, Jesus said, *"These things which you see—the days will come in which not one stone shall be left upon another that shall not be thrown down."* (Luke 21:6) After the Temple was destroyed, people did not know what to do or how to maintain a relationship with the Lord. Everything in their worship had been tied to the sacrificial system, but now there was no way to fulfill their religious duties.

On the other hand, those who received Jesus as the Lamb of God who took away the sins of the world knew exactly what they were called to do. They continued to fulfill the command of Jesus to carry the gospel to the world. The old Temple and the old Tabernacle were removed to make way for the new ones. *"The Holy Spirit was showing by this that the way into the Most Holy Place had not yet been disclosed as long as the first tabernacle was still standing."* (Hebrews 9:8, NIV) The true believers knew that the old Temple had been replaced by the new one which was now in their hearts. They could boldly say to new believers you are now the temple of God.

"Do you not know that you are the temple of God and that the Spirit of God dwells in you? If anyone defiles the temple of God, God will destroy him. For the temple of God is holy, which temple you are." (1 Corinthians 3:16-17)

This is a foundational doctrine of our faith. You are the temple of God and the sacrificial system has been fulfilled by Yeshua ha Messiach. It has happened just as Jesus prayed. All these things have been made available to those who believe through the teaching of the gospel. Therefore, this message is the Word of God for you. Study the passage below and receive it as God's Word given specifically for you. Now is the time to glorify God in our bodies and in our spirits.

"Or do you not know that your body is the temple of the Holy Spirit who is in you, whom you have from God, and you are not your own? For you were bought at a price; therefore glorify God in your body and in your spirit, which are God's." (1 Corinthians 6:19-20)

When the Holy Spirit occupies the temple in your body, He provides many things to help you with your walk of faith. Believers need to understand these things and learn how to access them. Have you ever gone through a time when you just didn't know what to do or even what to pray? Have you experienced a time when it seemed that you just didn't have the strength to finish the work which had been given to you? If you have gone through times like this or if you are experiencing these things right now, there is good news for you. The Holy Spirit has been sent to help with these very things.

> *"Likewise the Spirit also helps in our weaknesses. For we do not know what we should pray for as we ought, but the Spirit Himself makes intercession for us with groanings which cannot be uttered. Now He who searches the hearts knows what the mind of the Spirit is, because He makes intercession for the saints according to the will of God."* (Romans 8:26-27)

It would require a library of books to properly and completely explain all the ways the Holy Spirit works for us, in us, and through us. I have prepared a short list of these workings of the Holy Spirit below. Study them and seek to have all of them manifest in your life and ministry. These are all promises which you can claim as you faithfully follow and obey Jesus. As you study these, add content to make it your own. As you think of other things the Holy Spirit provides for you, add them to your list. This is a powerful way to build your faith and understanding.

1. The Holy Spirit enables you to know and preach the deep mysteries of the Word:

> *"To them it was revealed that, not to themselves, but to us they were ministering the things which now have been reported to you through those who have preached the gospel to you by the Holy Spirit sent from heaven—things which angels desire to look into."* (1 Peter 1:12)

165

2. The Holy Spirit enables you to prophesy:

"And so we have the prophetic word confirmed, which you do well to heed as a light that shines in a dark place, until the day dawns and the morning star rises in your hearts; knowing this first, that no prophecy of Scripture is of any private interpretation, for prophecy never came by the will of man, but holy men of God spoke as they were moved by the Holy Spirit." (2 Peter 1:19-21)

3. The Holy Spirit will speak through you:

"But when they arrest you and deliver you up, do not worry beforehand, or premeditate what you will speak. But whatever is given you in that hour, speak that; for it is not you who speak, but the Holy Spirit." (Mark 13:11)

4. The Holy Spirit works the miracles, signs and wonders:

"God also bearing witness both with signs and wonders, with various miracles, and gifts of the Holy Spirit, according to His own will?" (Hebrews 2:4)

5. The Holy Spirit makes us ready to access the Mercy Seat:

"But when the kindness and the love of God our Savior toward man appeared, not by works of righteousness which we have done, but according to His mercy He saved us, through the washing of regeneration and renewing of the Holy Spirit, whom He poured out on us abundantly through Jesus Christ our Savior," (Titus 3:4-6)

166

6. The Holy Spirit provides power to go along with the gospel we are called to preach:

"For our gospel did not come to you in word only, but also in power, and in the Holy Spirit and in much assurance, as you know what kind of men we were among you for your sake." (1 Thessalonians 1:5)

7. The Holy Spirit empowers our confession that Jesus is Lord:

"Therefore I make known to you that no one speaking by the Spirit of God calls Jesus accursed, and no one can say that Jesus is Lord except by the Holy Spirit." (1 Corinthians 12:3)

8. The Holy Spirit is the source of our Hope:

"Now hope does not disappoint, because the love of God has been poured out in our hearts by the Holy Spirit who was given to us." (Romans 5:5)

"Now may the God of hope fill you with all joy and peace in believing, that you may abound in hope by the power of the Holy Spirit." (Romans 15:13)

9. The Holy Spirit puts believers into offices of ministry:

"For I have not shunned to declare to you the whole counsel of God. Therefore take heed to yourselves and to all the flock, among which the Holy Spirit has made you overseers, to shepherd the church of God which He purchased with His own blood." (Acts 20:27-28)

10. The Holy Spirit is imparted through the laying on of hands:

"Then they laid hands on them, and they received the Holy Spirit." (Acts 8:17)

"And when Paul had laid hands on them, the Holy Spirit came upon them, and they spoke with tongues and prophesied." (Acts 19:6)

11. The Holy Spirit is our source of comfort

"Then the churches throughout all Judea, Galilee, and Samaria had peace and were edified. And walking in the fear of the Lord and in the comfort of the Holy Spirit, they were multiplied." (Acts 9:31)

12. The Holy Spirit directs the paths of our ministry:

"Now when they had gone through Phrygia and the region of Galatia, they were forbidden by the Holy Spirit to preach the word in Asia. After they had come to Mysia, they tried to go into Bithynia, but the Spirit did not permit them. So passing by Mysia, they came down to Troas. And a vision appeared to Paul in the night. A man of Macedonia stood and pleaded with him, saying, "Come over to Macedonia and help us." (Acts 16:6-9)

As I studied these passages of scripture, I started to notice all the different methods the Holy Spirit uses to speak to us. Paul had a vision in which the Holy Spirit released him to go to Macedonia to minister to the lost. Sometimes the Holy Spirit spoke to people in dreams. Other passages indicated that the Holy Spirit spoke to them in an audible voice. At other times, they heard it by the inner voice of their own spirits. All of these same methods are available for you to hear the Holy Spirit.

PRAYER

I pray for you to have more prophetic dreams, visions, and visitations. I pray for you to more clearly hear the voice of the Holy Spirit. I pray the prayer of Paul over you right now: '*And pray in the Spirit on all occasions with all kinds of prayers and requests. With this in mind, be alert and always keep on praying for all the saints. Pray also for me, that whenever I open my mouth, words may be given me so that I will fearlessly make known the mystery of the gospel, for which I am an ambassador in chains. Pray that I may declare it fearlessly, as I should.'"* (Ephesians 6:18-20, NIV)

SELAH QUESTIONS

1. How have you heard the Holy Spirit speaking into your life and ministry?

2. Think of a time when you received directions in ministry from the Holy Spirit. What did you hear and what did you do?

3. List the ways in which the Holy Spirit is working in your life.

4. In what specific ways is the Holy Spirit the foundation for your life and work in the kingdom of God?

5. What changed for you when the Holy Spirit made you His Temple?

CHAPTER 11

LEVEL 2: THE EMPOWERING GLORY

—∞∞—

"Then He said to them, "Thus it is written, and thus it was necessary for the Christ to suffer and to rise from the dead the third day, and that repentance and remission of sins should be preached in His name to all nations, beginning at Jerusalem. And you are witnesses of these things. Behold, I send the Promise of My Father upon you; but tarry in the city of Jerusalem until you are endued with power from on high." (Luke 24:46-49)

When Jesus spoke of the *"Promise of My Father,"* He was making reference to several different things which were going to be released on the day of Pentecost. In the previous chapter, we focused on the Holy Spirit filling the believers with His presence. That was and is one of the most awesome gifts of the Father. However, they were given much more on that day of outpouring. They received what Jesus spoke of in Luke Chapter Twenty-four. They received *"power from on high."* Those gathered in the Upper Room moved through the first two levels of glory in a very short period of time. This provides us with a very significant reminder that the Lord moves all things at His chosen speed and in His perfect timing.

We must also understand that His timing may be different for each individual believer. Our teaching must always acknowledge this truth. Even though all of this happened for them on the same day, you can still see that the levels of glory occurred in the same order the Lord revealed to me when I was instructed to write this book. The Lord is a master builder and He follows His own plans. He doesn't build the roof before He sets up the walls. He doesn't build the house and then put it on a foundation. He lays the solid foundation first and then builds on it in a systematic and organized way. As our spiritual house is being constructed, it also follows a set pattern. So, we see that the indwelling glory appears first as the chief cornerstone of our spiritual foundation.

Once the foundation is in place, the power gifts begin to flow. This stage is what I call "The Empowering Glory." I have studied the power gifts of the Spirit for many years and yet I keep learning new things almost daily. This is not upsetting for me. It is encouraging, because I am constantly excited about discovering what comes next. Every day I am ready for something new and exciting to happen in the spiritual realm. Today, I am expecting the Holy Spirit to release more power gifts for you and for me. Are you ready to receive them?

I am on an exciting adventure with the Holy Spirit, and I always want to know more, see more, and receive more of His gifts so that I can be a better servant. Over the last several years, I have been researching this idea of spiritual power, and want to share some of the results with you. Remember that this is an incomplete list. By the time this book is in print, I expect to know more and move to a higher level of His glory. Now, it is your turn. I pray that the Lord will guide you on this exciting adventure, and reveal more to you than I have yet been able to see and experience. I recommend that you add your own experiences and revelations to each of the sections below. Then take it further by adding new items to this list for your own record of what the Holy Spirit is doing in your life.

POWER FROM ON HIGH FOR YOU

"But you shall receive power when the Holy Spirit has come upon you; and you shall be witnesses to Me in Jerusalem, and in all Judea and Samaria, and to the end of the earth." (Acts 1:8)

1. GLORY BRINGS POWER TO WIN THE LOST

"And with many other words he testified and exhorted them, saying, 'Be saved from this perverse generation.' Then those who gladly received his word were baptized; and that day about three thousand souls were added to them." (Acts 2:40-41)

How would you like to see these results in your ministry? How would you like to receive that kind of power for your sermons and the lessons you teach? Imagine giving a sermon followed by 3,000 professions of faith in one day! That is really dramatic church growth. Notice that it came after they were imbued with "power from on high." It all comes from the power of God which He provides for you to win the lost and to literally make disciples of nations. I am praying for an outpouring like that again for you and for me.

"So continuing daily with one accord in the temple, and breaking bread from house to house, they ate their food with gladness and simplicity of heart, praising God and having favor with all the people. And the Lord added to the church daily those who were being saved." (Acts 2:46-47)

After thinking about these exciting possibilities, consider that every day more were added to their numbers. Imagine this kind of increase in your ministry. Think about more people being added to the membership of your church every day. The good news is that it didn't stop that day. It wasn't a onetime event which cannot be repeated. This power continued with them and it can flow continuously in you. With God, it just keeps getting better and better.

When the times got really challenging, they prayed for boldness to continue preaching the gospel. The Holy Spirit came upon them again with a fresh new baptism and released more power to them. *"And with great power the apostles gave witness to the resurrection of the Lord Jesus. And great grace was upon them all."* (Acts 4:33) This was the manifestation of what Jesus had spoken over them, and it empowered them to do what He had commanded. He gave them power to heal the sick and cast out demons. *"Then He appointed twelve, that they might be with Him and that He might send them out to preach, and to have power to heal sicknesses and to cast out demons:"* (Mark 3:14-15) This power is available for you right now. All you have to do is ask in faith in order to receive it.

2. GLORY BRINGS POWER WHICH RESULTS IN BELIEF:

"This beginning of signs Jesus did in Cana of Galilee, and manifested His glory; and His disciples believed in Him." (John 2:11)

Every manifestation of the glory of God releases a special gift of power to increase our belief. Every time the glory of God manifests, I find that my level of faith increases more and more. Moving from glory to glory is accompanied by this special gift of power from the Holy Spirit. Are you experiencing this in your own ministry? If not, I pray that "power from on high" will manifest for you right now, and you will begin to see these same results in your work for the Lord. John connects the concepts of power and belief as He explains the meaning of "the Word" becoming flesh.

"But as many as received him, to them gave he power to become the sons of God, even to them that believe on his name: Which were born, not of blood, nor of the will of the flesh, nor of the will of man, but of God." (John 1:12-13, KJV)

The first power given is for us to become "the sons of God." John quickly connects this with our beliefs. Which comes first: power or belief? Perhaps they both come at the same time. We need the power of the Holy Spirit to believe in Him before we can accept Him as our Messiah. Then power to believe flows from our acceptance of the gospel. These same two things will also move us from one level of glory to the next higher level. This is all about the power of God which He imparted in order to enable you to release His gifts of salvation and spiritual power. These are for all who believe in Jesus as the Son of God.

"Now to him that is of power to establish you according to my gospel, and the preaching of Jesus Christ, according to the revelation of the mystery, which was kept secret since the world began, But now is made manifest, and by the scriptures of the prophets, according to the commandment of the everlasting God, made known to all nations for the obedience of faith: To God only wise, be glory through Jesus Christ forever. Amen" (Romans 16:25-27, KJV)

3. GLORY AND POWER ARE CONNECTED IN GOD

"After these things I heard a loud voice of a great multitude in heaven, saying, "Alleluia! Salvation and glory and honor and power belong to the Lord our God!" (Revelation 19:1)

The more you look into these things, the more you become aware that you cannot separate power from glory. All of these amazing gifts (salvation, glory, honor, and power) are released in the weighty presence of His glory. You cannot spend time in the glory without these powerful attributes of God being transferred on to you. You must then hold firmly to all of these powerful gifts from God. They are the key to your ability to be an overcomer in time of tribulation.

"I am coming soon. Hold on to what you have, so that no one will take your crown. Him who overcomes I will make a pillar in the temple of my God. Never again will he leave it. I will write on him the name of my God and the name of the city of my God, the new Jerusalem, which is coming down out of heaven from my God; and I will also write on him my new name." (Revelation 3:11-12, NIV)

4. POWER FROM THE GLORY TO TRANSFORM YOU

"But we all, with unveiled face, beholding as in a mirror the glory of the Lord, are being transformed into the same image from glory to glory, just as by the Spirit of the Lord." (2 Corinthians 3:18)

When you encounter the glory of God, you will never be the same again. Unbelievers become obedient disciples. People consumed by fear are set free and receive the power to stand against whatever comes their way. Doubters become men and women of faith who are overcoming the world. The weak are made strong. The lost are found. All of those who are being moved by the glory are being so transformed that they are literally moving from glory to glory by the power of the Holy Spirit.

5. THE GLORY ESTABLISHS, STRENTHENS AND SETTLES

"But may the God of all grace, who called us to His eternal glory by Christ Jesus, after you have suffered a while, perfect, establish, strengthen, and settle you." (1 Peter 5:10)

As you spend time in the glory and experience the transformation it provides, you will find yourself being changed in some wonderful ways. People spend the most part of their early years working to be established in the world. With all of their work and struggles, they often find themselves more unsettled than ever. Jobs come and go. Worldly favor can be lost in a moment. Public opinion is fickle and can fade in an instant. The only way to be truly settled and firmly established is by receiving and trusting in what the Lord has for you. You don't have to work for it. It is a free gift from the Lord which is released in abundance to those who spend time in His glory.

When you are established and settled in the Lord, you are also strengthened by His might. Joel prophesied this, *"Let the weak say, 'I am strong.'"* (Joel 3:10) The only way to legitimately do this is by drawing strength from the Lord. The good news is that He is willing to freely give it. When you decree in faith that you are strong, it is amazing what the Lord will do. Try it! I have done it many times. I begin to say over and over with increasing confidence, *"I am strong!"* and strength always comes. Paul knew something about this and prayed it over the Ephesians. He prayed for them to be strengthened with *"power."*

"I pray that out of his glorious riches he may strengthen you with power through his Spirit in your inner being, so that Christ may dwell in your hearts through faith. And I pray that you, being rooted and established in love, may

have power, together with all the saints, to grasp how wide and long and high and deep is the love of Christ, and to know this love that surpasses knowledge—that you may be filled to the measure of all the fullness of God." (Ephesians 3:16-19, NIV)

6. RESURRECTION POWER RELEASED IN THE GLORY.

"Or do you not know that as many of us as were baptized into Christ Jesus were baptized into His death? Therefore we were buried with Him through baptism into death, that just as Christ was raised from the dead by the glory of the Father, even so we also should walk in newness of life." (Romans 6:3-4)

What kind of power did Paul expect people to receive from the Lord? He wanted them to receive power for a new life. He prayed for them to receive a spiritual resurrection which took them beyond death to eternal life even while they remained on the Earth. Paul asserts that Christ was raised from the dead by "the glory of the Father." Remember that Jesus prayed for you to have the same glory the Father gave to Him.

There is resurrection power in the glory of the Father. Using this glory, Jesus raised several people from the dead. Later, Jesus himself was raised by this power of the glory. Now get this! He commanded us to walk in the same level of glory. Are you ready for this? He commanded us to raise the dead.

"Heal the sick, cleanse the lepers, raise the dead, cast out demons. Freely you have received, freely give." (Matthew 10:8)

7. GLORY RLEASES REVELATION KNOWLEDGE

"To them God willed to make known what are the riches of the glory of this mystery among the Gentiles: which is Christ in you, the hope of glory." (Colossians 1:27)

There are many things which can only be made known in the glory. In a glory outpouring in Korea, I was struggling to teach what I believed was a very simple point, but the people were not receiving it. I asked the Lord what I should do. Then I heard the voice of God say, "There are some things you can only teach in the glory!" I immediately received this word and prayed for the glory to fall on all of us so the people could receive the message. The glory fell and everyone when down under the weight of His glory, and I couldn't teach anything at that point. As I worked to understand this, it came to me in the Spirit. Some things can only be taught by the Holy Spirit when people are under the power of His glory.

"…the eyes of your understanding being enlightened; that you may know what is the hope of His calling, what are the riches of the glory of His inheritance in the saints," (Ephesians 1:18)

8. GOD'S GLORY LITERALLY ILLUMINATES

"The city had no need of the sun or of the moon to shine in it, for the glory of God illuminated it. The Lamb is its light." (Revelation 21:23)

When Moses spent time in the glory, it was transferred to him and his face literally glowed with the glory of God which was on him. Think about it. If Moses was still glowing, how much more was this glow flowing from the glory of the Lord. This is the strong message in the passage from Revelation Chapter 21.

The Father glows with such intensity that He will provide all the light for the new Heaven and the New Earth. Jesus will also be a light in that time. The disciples saw how that was possible when they beheld His glory on the Mount of Transfiguration. The Lord gave me a vision of the intensity of the light of His glory.

(A Vision of the Glory)

This morning, the Lord began to fill the room where I was worshipping with angels. They were the kind I call "Angels of Fire," because their appearance is like a consuming fire. They are amber in color and seem to be burning without being consumed. As the angels appeared one after another in the room, I began to say to each one, "I release you to minister what The Lord sent you to minister!" My hands began to be covered and filled with vibrations and fire. I felt a sensation in my hand like being stuck by a large needle. I always feel this sensation when the Spirit of Holiness is present.

I sensed that many new spiritual gifts were being released and that there was an increase in the anointing for spiritual gifts I had previously received. Then a strong anointing for healing came to both of my hands and I started to release it to myself and to others in intercession. As I interceded for others, it felt like the fire in my hands was increasing in strength. Then I suddenly felt fire on both my face and hands as I imparted the gifts and the anointing from the Lord to others in prayer.

I was suddenly startled, because I was taken in the Spirit to a heavenly place at an extremely fast speed. My startle response brought me out of the experience instantly. I repented for my reaction, and prayed to return to that place. I only got a few glimpses of it. Each time I could see the reflection of a powerful fire on the wall in front of me. I sensed that I was in the presence of the glory of God, but it was too strong for me to look directly at it. So, I just soaked in it. I was open to receive everything the Spirit would release to me in the time I spent in the glory! I sensed that my experience of His Presence was growing stronger and stronger. I knew that His Presence always comes in full power, but I was experiencing it as an increase because my ability to perceive it was being increased more and more.

At this point, I felt another increase in the release of spiritual gifts and the anointing from the Spirit of holiness and the many holiness angels in the room. Then I was carried by the Spirit back to the resourcing room in Heaven. Several people were there with me this morning. Perhaps you were there with us. We were each given very large bags like the huge leaf bags used outdoors to clean up the lawn. We were each filling the bags to overflowing with spiritual gifts and healing gifts.

By revelation knowledge from the Holy Spirit, I understood that we are in a season to receive more than enough to deal with everything the enemy is trying to work against us. We are receiving an increase in spiritual authority to minister the gifts of the Spirit in this season. Remember the Lord's promise in Luke 10:19, *"Behold, I give you the authority to trample on serpents and scorpions, and over all the power of the enemy, and nothing shall by any means hurt you."*

The Lord is pouring out more resources than the enemy can steal. My thoughts went back to John 10:10, *"The thief does not come except to steal, and to kill, and to destroy. I have come that they may have life, and that they may have it more abundantly."* Are you ready for some abundance from the Lord? Now is the time to reach out and take it! I just continued to soak in it and allow the Spirit to give as much as He was willing to release. Father God, thank you! Thank you! Thank you!

I received a powerful assurance from the Lord again this morning, "Do not be anxious or afraid! I am with you and you have nothing to fear! I am your provider! Stay close to Me and I will stay close to you!" Amen! Even so, come quickly Lord Jesus!

I pray that you will also see the magnificent fire of His glory and experience all of these things and more. May you receive all the Lord is releasing for your life and ministry today as He manifests His awesome glory for you! May the Lord give you increase more and more (Psalm 115:14)! May you be empowered to face every challenge! May you be anointed to minister more powerfully in all the gifts of the Spirit! Amen and 3Amen!

(End of Vision)

In the Last days, this glory glow will also come from certain angels sent by the Lord. *"After these things I saw another angel coming down from heaven, having great authority, and the earth was illuminated with his glory."* (Rev 18:1) The glory of God on this angel will illuminate the earth. As you study the passages above, try to imagine the glory of the Father glowing on your face. Is that possible? I believe it is and that it will soon manifest. As you spend time with Him, it will be transferred to you. The glow on people fades because it is not coming from them. To keep the glow, you must spend a great deal of time with the Lord. So, why aren't you glowing now? You must believe it to receive it, and you must spend more time with Him in His glory.

9. GLORY PROVIDES A COVERING

"...then the Lord will create above every dwelling place of Mount Zion, and above her assemblies, a cloud and smoke by day and the shining of a flaming fire by night. For over all the glory there will be a covering." (Isaiah 4:5)

The word Isaiah received from the Lord speaks of two powerful realities which the children of Israel experienced in the wilderness. There was a covering over the glory of God in the Tabernacle, and there was a covering from His glory over them. The cloud of His glory accompanied them as they traveled and in the camps they set up. It provided a great sense of security and protection for them as it shielded them from danger.

The column of fire at night illuminated their camp and reminded them that they were covered and protected by the power of His glory. Isaiah released a powerful word of prophecy which declared that this same covering will return to rest above every dwelling. This promise was specifically for Israel, but it is also for you and me. I like to visualize that glow of His glory illuminating our world as I pray for it to manifest in our generation. If you think it is possible, begin to pray for it and expect it so that it can manifest. Amen?

10. THE GLORY IS YOUR REAR GUARD

"Then your light shall break forth like the morning, your healing shall spring forth speedily, and your righteousness shall go before you; The glory of the Lord shall be your rear guard." (Isaiah 58:8)

Do you need a "rear guard?" I believe we all need this level of the Lord's protection. Notice that the healing of the Lord is always for spirit, soul, and body. The light of His glory provides healing for your body and for your soul. Then it provides the Lord's gift of righteousness to heal your spirit. We all have blind spots. We do not have eyes in the back of our heads. We need someone to stand behind us and protect us from all danger. The glory of the Lord provides all you need. Expect it in your own life and ministry.

11. THE GLORY CAUSES ENEMIES TO FEAR

"So shall they fear the name of the Lord from the west, and His glory from the rising of the sun; When the enemy comes in like a flood, the Spirit of the Lord will lift up a standard against him." (Isaiah 59:19)

The enemies of the Lord fear His glory. They cannot stand in His presence. The light of His glory exposes every hidden thing including every demonic hold on people. The enemy may seem to be coming in strong, but he doesn't stand a chance when the glory appears. *"These shall be punished with everlasting destruction from the presence of the Lord and from the glory of His power,"* (2 Thessalonians 1:9) Let the Holy Spirit come to you in the power of His glory and establish a standard to protect you, your family, and your church. When the glory comes, the Holy Spirit arms us with spiritual weapons.

> *"For the weapons of our warfare are not carnal but mighty in God for pulling down strongholds, casting down arguments and every high thing that exalts itself against the knowledge of God, bringing every thought into captivity to the obedience of Christ, and being ready to punish all disobedience when your obedience is fulfilled."* (2 Corinthians 10:4-6)

All of these things have been provided for you and they still flow from the glory of the Father. Remember that Jesus was the express representation of the glory of God. He carried it in fullness. His life is a model for us. Remember what Jesus said in John 14:12, *"Most assuredly, I say to you, he who believes in Me, the works that I do he will do also; and greater works than these he will do, because I go to My Father."* Are you expecting to do greater works than Jesus did on the earth? If not, ask yourself if you are truly being obedient to Him? We need to walk in a greater level of authority and in the power of His glory! Consider this as you study the passage below from the King James Version of the Bible. The focus here is on the gift of power rather than authority.

"Behold, I give unto you power to tread on serpents and scorpions, and over all the power of the enemy: and nothing shall by any means hurt you." (Luke 10:19, KJV)

12. GLORY IS THE ANSWER TO DEEP DARKNESS

How dark is it in your world right now? Does it sometimes seem that the darkness is getting stronger and thicker? Have you already reached the level of *"deep darkness?"* If you are in deep darkness right now, I have good news for you! The glory of the Father and of the Son has risen upon you! This glory has and will continue to overcome the darkness, and it will be seen by others upon you!

"Arise, shine; for your light has come! And the glory of the Lord is risen upon you. For behold, the darkness shall cover the earth, and deep darkness the people; But the Lord will arise over you, and His glory will be seen upon you." (Isaiah 60:1-2)

13. THE GLORY ENABLES YOU TO WALK WORTHY

"For you know that we dealt with each of you as a father deals with his own children, encouraging, comforting and urging you to live lives worthy of God, who calls you into his kingdom and glory." (1 Thessalonians 2:11-12, NIV)

We will never be good enough from our own works to be called worthy. We will never be able to claim that we are righteous because of what we have accomplished. We have all fallen short of the glory of God, but the story doesn't end there. We have been called *"into his kingdom and glory."* As we enter into His kingdom and His glory, we are declared righteous by what Jesus has done for us. He has done what we could never do. Now, He is inviting us into the glory realm so that we can receive it and have confidence and assurance of His grace and salvation.

14. GLORY GIVES US AN ETERNAL PERSPECTIVE

"For our light affliction, which is but for a moment, is working for us a far more exceeding and eternal weight of glory, while we do not look at the things which are seen, but at the things which are not seen. For the things which are seen are temporary, but the things which are not seen are eternal." (2 Corinthians 4:17-18)

When I was stationed in Korea as an Army Chaplain, I went through a very stress filled period of time. To deal with it, I took a one day vacation from the stress and strain of my work, and climbed to the top of a beautiful mountain. On a majestic mountain peak, I sat down and gazed out across miles and miles of God's awesome creation. As I sat and admired the glory of His amazing creation, something in me was transformed. All the stress and anxiety evaporated. As I came down the mountain, I realized that my perspective had dramatically shifted. From time to time, we all need to go higher in the Lord where we can get a new perspective on our lives and the struggles we face. As we are lifted up higher and higher in His glory, our afflictions seem light and our troubles seem to only last for a few moments. I call these experiences "glory breaks."

Do you need a glory break today? All you have to do is, *"Enter into His gates with thanksgiving, and into His courts with praise. Be thankful to Him, and bless His name."* (Psalm 100:4) Think back over the fourteen kinds of power I have listed for you, and give thanks to the Lord for all He is providing for you in His glory. Give thanks that you have been lifted up into this amazing and empowering level of His glory. I pray that you will discover ways to maintain the presence, power and glory of God in your life!

PRAYER

"As You sent Me into the world, I also have sent them into the world. And for their sakes I sanctify Myself, that they also may be sanctified by the truth. I do not pray for these alone, but also for those who will believe in Me through their word; that they all may be one, as You, Father, are in Me, and I in You; that they also may be one in Us, that the world may believe that You sent Me. And the glory which You gave Me I have given them, that they may be one just as We are one: I in them, and You in Me; that they may be made perfect in one, and that the world may know that You have sent Me, and have loved them as You have loved Me. Father, I desire that they also whom You gave Me may be with Me where I am, that they may behold My glory which You have given Me; for You loved Me before the foundation of the world." (John 17:18-24)

SELAH QUESTIONS

1. In what ways have you experienced the empowering level of His glory?

2. Look over the fourteen ways you can receive power in the glory, and list those you have personally experienced.

3. Think about your current needs and which of these types of empowerment you need. Then ask the Lord to provide these for you. List them in the space below:

4. Are you actively seeking His glory? What are some of the ways you are doing this?

5. List below any other types of empowerment the Lord has revealed to you.

CHAPTER 12

LEVEL 3: THE GIFTING GLORY

"There are different kinds of gifts, but the same Spirit. There are different kinds of service, but the same Lord. There are different kinds of working, but the same God works all of them in all men. Now to each one the manifestation of the Spirit is given for the common good." (1Corinthians 12:4-7, NIV)

THE GLORY MOVES US BEYOND OURSELVES

"Even so you, since you are zealous for spiritual gifts, let it be for the edification of the church that you seek to excel." (1 Corinthians 14:12)

Spiritual gifts are always given for a purpose. They are not given to make you rich, beautiful, attractive, famous or popular. Remember: It is not all about you. Gifts are given to take you beyond yourself so that you can serve the Lord. Gifts are given to help you focus on others and their needs, dreams, and desires. Gifts are given so that you can help build up the body of Christ and strengthen it for the fulfillment of its destiny in Christ Jesus. Your zeal needs to focus more on the body of Christ than on the gifts you want to receive. When you obediently step out to accomplish the work of the Lord, the gifts of the

Spirit flow to make it happen. This will always remind you to keep your focus on Him and on your mission to advance the kingdom of God.

> *"But the manifestation of the Spirit is given to each one for the profit of all: for to one is given the word of wisdom through the Spirit, to another the word of knowledge through the same Spirit, to another faith by the same Spirit, to another gifts of healings by the same Spirit, to another the working of miracles, to another prophecy, to another discerning of spirits, to another different kinds of tongues, to another the interpretation of tongues. But one and the same Spirit works all these things, distributing to each one individually as He wills."* (1 Corinthians 12:7-11)

The gifts are given to individuals in order to profit all the members of the body of Christ. As you study the nature of these spiritual gifts, this truth is made very clear. You receive words of wisdom and words of knowledge so that you can minister healing, deliverance, and grace to those in need. You are given the gift of faith in order to release the power of God in your ministry of preaching, teaching, and healing. Miracles, healings, signs and wonders accompany the proclamation of the gospel to convince unbelievers and release faith in them. The same is true of all the spiritual gifts. They are given for the profit of all.

FOUR TYPES OF GIFTING

> *"Now you are the body of Christ, and members individually. And God has appointed these in the church: first apostles, second prophets, third teachers, after that miracles, then gifts of healings, helps, administrations, varieties of tongues."* (1 Corinthians 12:27-28)

It is very interesting that Paul provides two lists of spiritual gifts in the twelfth chapter of First Corinthians. It is also fascinating that the lists are slightly different. In the passage above gifts and offices of ministry are mixed together with this second list of gifts. The list of offices is also different from the list in the fourth chapter of Ephesians. I believe this list was given to expand on the others as well as to give them context within the body of Christ. With this in view, the new items in this list are to be added to the list at the beginning of the chapter in the same way you would add an afterthought. The list below is my attempt to do that very thing.

POWER GIFTS GIVEN IN THE GLORY

1. THE SPIRITUAL GIFT OF FAITH:

"…to another faith by the same Spirit," (1 Corinthians 12:9)

The Spiritual gift of faith is the supernatural ability to believe beyond all doubt. This is not the natural response from people. Most people want to see something first and then believe in it. Supernatural faith believes without first seeing. For example supernatural faith is seen when someone has faith to be healed before any healing begins to occur. The person with this kind of faith has already received it by faith and is simply waiting for it to manifest. Notice how faith and grace work together in the passage below.

> *"For by grace you have been saved through faith, and that not of yourselves; it is the gift of God, not of works, lest anyone should boast."* (Ephesians 2:8-9)

It is this saving grace through faith which gets you into the Kingdom of God. This is a power gift because it produces fruit. One spiritual fruit from this kind of faith is to gradually get the

Kingdom of God into you. This appropriating of the Kingdom of God is truly a work of the gift of faith. The gift of faith combines both kinds of faith (saving faith and fruit producing faith) and then goes one more step. The gift of faith receives the answer before it is manifested.

2. THE GIFTS OF HEALINGS

"...to another gifts of healings by the same Spirit" (1 Corinthians 12:9)

First, notice that both key words are plural. There are many different gifts and many types of healings. All of the spiritual gifts of healings are supernatural. They are done with no human assistance. The most obvious type is physical healings. Things like diabetes, blindness, cancer, deafness, and etc. are completely healed when this spiritual gift is released. Many of these types of healings are recorded in both the Old and New Testaments of the Bible. The second major category is emotional healings. Things like jealousy, worry, discouragement, and other destructive attitudes. The third major category is spiritual healing. When this occurs, we see spiritual issues like unforgiveness, bitterness, self-condemnation, greed, guilt, and etc. come under the power of God through the ministry of a gift of healing. The gifts are given for a variety of purposes. The preaching of the Word of God is confirmed through these signs. Another positive outcome occurs when people are healed or see others receive healing and then glorify God. The working of these healing gifts helps build faith in the people who witness them. As you study the healings recorded in the Bible, begin to make a list of these outcomes and let them strengthen your own faith.

3. WORKING OF MIRACLES

"...to another the working of miracles" (1 Corinthians 12:10)

The word *miracle* comes from the Greek word "*dunamis*." This is the root of many words such as dynamo, dynamic, dynamite, and etc. The word "dunamis" is defined as power or might which multiplies itself. Miracles witnessed to the divinity of Yeshua ha Messiach: "*But I have a greater witness than John's; for the works which the Father has given Me to finish—the very works that I do—bear witness of Me, that the Father has sent Me.*" (John 5:36) Miracles resulted in people believing the Gospel. "*And the multitudes with one accord heeded the things spoken by Philip, hearing and seeing the miracles which he did.*" (Acts 8:6)

This is the kind of work we are commissioned to do. "*Most assuredly, I say to you, he who believes in Me, the works that I do he will do also; and greater works than these he will do, because I go to My Father.*" (John 14:12) If we are being obedient to Christ and ministering in accordance with His Word and His commandments, we should be see miracles continuously. This power was not taken away from the body of Christ. The working of miracles may have been neglected and even forgotten at times, but it is not because the Lord is withholding these promised spiritual gifts. It is time for us to get back to the basics of our calling. Remember what Jesus commanded: "*Heal the sick, cleanse the lepers, raise the dead, cast out demons. Freely you have received, freely give.*" (Matthew 10:8)

REVELATION GIFTS GIVEN IN THE GLORY

1. THE WORD OF WISDOM

"...for to one is given the word of wisdom through the Spirit" (1 Corinthians 12:8)

"Therefore settle it in your hearts not to meditate before-hand on what you will answer; for I will give you a mouth and wisdom which all your adversaries will not be able to contradict or resist." (Luke 21:14-15)

There are at least three types of wisdom referenced in the Word of God. There is of course the wisdom of God, but there are also references to the wisdom of the world (natural or fleshly), and the wisdom of man (ability to reason). When we speak of the "word of wisdom" which is a gift of the Holy Spirit, it should be clear that this is totally about the wisdom of God which has been made available to you and to me. This wisdom supernaturally helps us to know what to say, what to do, when to do it, and how to do what the Lord calls us to accomplish in ministry. How do you get this kind of wisdom? It is so simple. All you have to do is place a claim on the promises in the Word of God and ask. *"If any of you lacks wisdom, let him ask of God, who gives to all liberally and without reproach, and it will be given to him."* (James 1:5)

2. THE WORD OF KNOWLEDGE.

"...to another the word of knowledge through the same Spirit" (1 Corinthians 12:8)

This is not a reference to the normal idea of gaining knowledge through study and memorization. The knowledge referenced here is a special gift of the Holy Spirit. It is the

194

sudden and supernatural understanding of situations, problems, and facts needed to fulfill your purpose in the Kingdom of God. It is the revelation of the divine will and purposes of God for you, your family, and the church. Why does the Lord do this? *"For this is good and acceptable in the sight of God our Savior, who desires all men to be saved and to come to the knowledge of the truth."* (1 Timothy 2:3-4) This gift is given so that you can be more effective in your ministry preaching, teaching and administrating the other gifts of the Spirit. This is one of the primary ways the Holy Spirit leads us.

3. THE DISCERNING OF SPIRITS.

"...to another discerning of spirits" (1 Corinthians 12:10)

This gift has to do with judging by evidence whether spirits are of God or not. It is the gift which allows us to choose wisely who we will listen to and who we will allow to impart things to us. It is the Spiritual gift which helps us to make good choices about what we will possess and use in our lives and ministries. It is the very special gift to know the enemy and see the movement of his wicked spirits. So, it also involves knowing by revelation the plans and activities of the enemy. This is God's way of protecting us. Study the three passages below and learn well the lessons of the Scriptures given to guide us in the proper use of this priceless and powerful gift of the Holy Spirit:

> *"And this I pray, that your love may abound still more and more in knowledge and all discernment, that you may approve the things that are excellent, that you may be sincere and without offense till the day of Christ, being filled with the fruits of righteousness which are by Jesus Christ, to the glory and praise of God."* (Philippians 1:9-11)

"Folly is joy to him who is destitute of discernment, but a man of understanding walks uprightly." (Proverbs 15:21)

"Yes, if you cry out for discernment, and lift up your voice for understanding, If you seek her as silver, and search for her as for hidden treasures; then you will understand the fear of the Lord, and find the knowledge of God." (Proverbs 2:3-5)

VOCAL GIFTS GIVEN IN THE GLORY

1. THE SPIRITUAL GIFT OF PROPHECY

"...to another prophecy" (1 Corinthians 12:10)

The word "prophecy" is from the Greek word *"propheteuo."* This Greek word means to "speak for another." It literally means to be God's spokesperson (ambassador). We are told to desire and to operate in this gift of the Spirit. *"Pursue love, and desire spiritual gifts, but especially that you may prophesy."* (1 Corinthians 14:1) It is speaking under the inspiration of God. We must not stifle the release of this spiritual gift. *"Do not quench the Spirit. Do not despise prophecies."* (1 Thessalonians 5:19-20) True prophesy always exalts Jesus as Savior and Lord! *"For the testimony of Jesus is the spirit of prophecy."* (Revelation 19:10c)

There are at least four reasons why prophecy is important in the church. Prophesy is given to build us up. It is to challenge us to do the work of the Gospel. It is to give us comfort because of God's love. Prophesy should be a common gift in the church. These four purposes are:

- FIRST: It brings life. Prophecy brought life to the valley of dry bones. (Ezekiel 37:1-4)

- SECOND: It edifies, exhorts, and comforts: "But he who prophesies speaks edification and exhortation and comfort to men." (I Corinthians 14:3)
- THIRD: It brings revival and restoration. (See Acts 2:16-18)
- FOURTH: It is used by God to direct you where to go. (See Acts 13:1-3)

2. THE SPIRITUAL GIFT OF SPEAKING IN TONGUES

"...to another *different* kinds of tongues" (1 Corinthians 12:10)

This is an often misunderstood gift. Many churches forbid the speaking in tongues. But we must remember what is taught in the Word of God: *"Therefore, brethren, desire earnestly to prophesy, and do not forbid to speak with tongues."* (1 Corinthians 14:39) Paul makes it very clear in the fourteenth chapter of Firsts Corinthians that there is a place for the diversity of tongues in the body of Christ. How should we understand it? Begin my understanding that everything broken in the fall of man in the Garden of Eden is corrected through Christ. After mankind was put out of the Garden things began to go downhill in their relationship with the Lord. At the Tower of Babel, they were given a diversity of tongues which separated them to limit the evil they could do. On the Day of Pentecost another diversity of tongues was given. This time the diversity of tongues brought people together, and restored an old connection with God. *"For he who speaks in a tongue does not speak to men but to God, for no one understands him; however, in the spirit he speaks mysteries."* (1 Corinthians 14:2)

1. THIS TYPE OF TONGUE EDIFIES THE BELIEVER.

"He who speaks in a tongue edifies himself" (1 Corinthians 14:4)

197

2. THIS TYPE OF TONGUE ASSISTS YOU IN PRAYER

"Likewise the Spirit also helps in our weaknesses. For we do not know what we should pray for as we ought, but the Spirit Himself makes intercession for us with groanings which cannot be uttered. Now He who searches the hearts knows what the mind of the Spirit is, because He makes intercession for the saints according to the will of God." (Romans 8:26-27)

3. THIS TYPE OF TONGUE STIRS UP THE PRO- PHETIC MINISTRY

"I wish you all spoke with tongues, but even more that you prophesied; for he who prophesies is greater than he who speaks with tongues, unless indeed he interprets, that the church may receive edification." (1 Corinthians 14:5)

4. THIS TYPE OF TONGUE REFRESHES YOUR SOUL

"For with stammering lips and another tongue He will speak to this people, to whom He said, "This is the rest with which you may cause the weary to rest," and, "This is the refreshing"; yet they would not hear." (Isaiah 28:11-12)

5. THIS TYPE OF TONGUE GIVES VICTORY OVER THE DEVIL

"For he who speaks in a tongue does not speak to men but to God, for no one understands him; however, in the spirit he speaks mysteries." (1 Corinthians 14:2)

"...praying always with all prayer and supplication in the Spirit," (Ephesians 6:18)

6. TONGUES HELP YOU WORSHIP IN THE SPIRIT

*"For if I pray in a tongue, my spirit prays, but my under-
standing is unfruitful. What is the conclusion then? I
will pray with the spirit, and I will also pray with the
understanding. I will sing with the spirit, and I will also
sing with the understanding."* (1 Corinthians 14:14-15)

THE GIFT OF INTERPRETATION OF TONGUES

"...to another the interpretation of tongues." (1 Corinthians 12:10)

The word "interpretation" in this passage is from the Greek
word "*harmeneia.*" It is defined as "explanation" or "full interpretation." It means to give the meaning of words spoken with
tongues. This gift is given by the Holy Spirit to edify the church.
You can clearly see this in 1 Corinthians 14:16, *"Otherwise, if
you bless with the spirit, how will he who occupies the place
of the uninformed say "Amen" at your giving of thanks, since
he does not understand what you say?"* Interpretation may be
given by the one who speaks in tongues or by another person
who has received this spiritual gift.

Everything is to be done in good order for the benefit of all.
One aspect of good order is to be certain that someone interprets
a tongue to make it clear to all the others. 1 Corinthians 14:27,
*"If anyone speaks in a tongue, let there be two or at the most
three, each in turn, and let one interpret."* Otherwise, the gift
will not edify and bless the body of Christ. If not interpreted, it
will confuse people rather than serve to build them up.

It is appropriate for all believers to pray for this spiritual gift.
Both the one who is speaking and the ones who are listening
should pray for the gift of interpretation. Who does Paul say
should speak with tongues? The answer is that everyone should
be able to use this gift. In addition, all who speak with tongues

should pray for the gift of interpretation. 1 Corinthians 14:13, *"Therefore let him who speaks in a tongue pray that he may interpret."* Therefore, it is appropriate to pray for it. And according to Paul we should all pray for both gifts. Below is a summary of things you learn from Paul's teachings in 1 Corinthians chapters twelve and fourteen:

1) The gift of interpretation of tongues is for the Church.
2) This gift is necessary in order to edify all who hear it.
3) This gift was never taken out of the Church.
4) This gift has been available down through church history.
5) Paul taught the church at Corinth to use this gift.

ADMINISTRATIVE GIFTS GIVEN IN THE GLORY

"And God has appointed these in the church: first apostles, second prophets, third teachers, after that miracles, then gifts of healings, helps, administrations, varieties of tongues." (1 Corinthians 12:28)

1. THE SPIRITUAL GIFT OF "HELPS"

The Greek word Paul used in the passage above, which was translated as helps is "antilepsis." It is referring to people who help the sick, the aged, the widowed, the poor, and the needy. It is a gift of divine love placed in the hearts of men and women to commit their lives to help those who either cannot or are limited in their ability to care for themselves. This spiritual gift first manifested in those chosen to care for the widows in the early church.

"Now in those days, when the number of the disciples was multiplying, there arose a complaint against the Hebrews by the Hellenists, because their widows were neglected in the daily distribution. Then the twelve summoned the

multitude of the disciples and said, "It is not desirable that we should leave the word of God and serve tables. Therefore, brethren, seek out from among you seven men of good reputation, full of the Holy Spirit and wisdom, whom we may appoint over this business; but we will give ourselves continually to prayer and to the ministry of the word." (Acts 6:1-4)

Those selected for this purpose were called deacons and their ministry was the administration of "helps" for the members of the body of Christ who were widows. Notice the qualifications for this position. These requirements sound more like the characteristics for a pastor or evangelist. They had to have a good reputation and be filled with the Holy Spirit to be qualified for the assignment. They needed the wisdom of God and of the Holy Spirit to do their jobs correctly. This was clearly viewed as a high office in the early church. Remember what Jesus taught and modeled: *"If I then, your Lord and Teacher, have washed your feet, you also ought to wash one another's feet. For I have given you an example, that you should do as I have done to you."* (John 13:14-15) We should honor, respect, and bless those who are given this wonderful gift of "helps."

2. THE SPIRITUAL GIFT OF "ADMINISTRATIONS"

   a. A gift to administer justice: 1 Kings 3:28, Ezra 7:25, Jeremiah 21:12
   b. A gift to righteously administer judgment: Psalm 9:8, 2 Chronicles 19:8
   c. A gift for properly managing offerings to honor the Lord: 2 Corinthians 8:19
   d. A gift to avoid criticism for mishandling money: 2 Corinthians 8:20

THE GLORY MAKES YOU FRUITFUL

"Then God blessed them, and God said to them, "Be fruitful and multiply; fill the earth and subdue it; have dominion over the fish of the sea, over the birds of the air, and over every living thing that moves on the earth." (Genesis 1:28)

It was God's plan from the beginning for all His people to be fruitful and to multiply. In fact, He commanded it to the first man and woman. The task was huge then, and it is still very big today. We don't need to populate the world any more, but we do need to populate the kingdom of God. This task seems to be larger than merely reproducing to fill the Earth. As soon as sin came into the world, people were in bondage to it. People who are in bondage to sin have difficulty being set free from it. The deception of sin is so great that many people willingly choose to stay in it. How will they ever be set free?

On your best day, you are not up to the task based on your own gifts and abilities. You need something more: much more! You need the full gifting of God and the power of His glory to advance the Kingdom of God. When people have relied on their own power over the centuries, the church has not made much progress. However the command of the Lord is still valid for you and me, and it is time for the body of Christ to subdue the Earth and have dominion over it and every living thing on the planet.

"But the fruit of the Spirit is love, joy, peace, longsuffering, kindness, goodness, faithfulness, gentleness, self-control. Against such there is no law." (Galatians 5:22-23)

In this season of our service for the Kingdom, I believe this is directly related to the Lord's command for us to be fruitful. We are to produce the "fruit of the Spirit" in abundance so that there will be a bumper crop for the Kingdom of God. This task is so overwhelming that we need to get into the glory and be empowered and gifted to do it. I have learned this lesson: We need the gifts of the Spirit in order to produce the fruit of the Spirit.

GIFTS IMPARTED IN THE GLORY

"For I long to see you, that I may impart to you some spiritual gift, so that you may be established—that is, that I may be encouraged together with you by the mutual faith both of you and me." (Romans 1:11-12)

The gifts of the Spirit all belong to the Holy Spirit, and He distributes them according to His will and the will of the Father. In this passage, Paul is not claiming to have his own gifts to impart to others. He is actually making a strong affirmation that the Lord has chosen to let him be the instrument through which the Holy Spirit imparts these gifts. Paul was always faithful to follow the leadership of the Holy Spirit. Therefore, he could confidently announce that he had some spiritual gift to impart. I am also confident that Paul had received this as a word of knowledge from the Holy Spirit.

If we are to be faithful in imparting gifts, we must also commit to do only those things the Holy Spirit directs us to do. Remember how Jesus worked! *"And I know that His command is everlasting life. Therefore, whatever I speak, just as the Father has told Me, so I speak."* (John 12:50) Like Jesus, we are to do what we see the Father doing and speak what we hear the Father saying. How do we see the Father? The key is in John 14:9, *"Jesus said to him, "Have I been with you so long, and yet you have not known Me, Philip? He who has seen Me has seen the Father; so how can you say, 'Show us the Father'?"* We must keep our eyes fixed on Jesus, and He will reveal all these things to us. Study the passage below and let these truths sink deep into your spirit and soul.

*"Then Jesus answered and said to them, "Most assuredly,
I say to you, the Son can do nothing of Himself, but what
He sees the Father do; for whatever He does, the Son
also does in like manner. For the Father loves the Son,
and shows Him all things that He Himself does; and He
will show Him greater works than these, that you may
marvel. For as the Father raises the dead and gives life
to them, even so the Son gives life to whom He will."*
(John 5:19-21)

NO SHORTAGE OF GIFTING IN THE GLORY

*"For in him you have been enriched in every way—in all
your speaking and in all your knowledge—because our
testimony about Christ was confirmed in you. Therefore
you do not lack any spiritual gift as you eagerly wait for
our Lord Jesus Christ to be revealed. He will keep you
strong to the end, so that you will be blameless on the day
of our Lord Jesus Christ."* (1 Corinthians 1:5-8, NIV)

There is no problem of lack in the kingdom economy. There
are no shortages of any of the things we need for our walk with
the Lord. He never runs short of gifts to give and blessings
to release. There is no legitimate reason for us to lack any
of the spiritual gifts. If there is a problem with receiving, we
can always trace it back to ourselves. We have likely stepped
outside the blessing flow because of some area of resistance
or rebellion in our own spirits. However, there is more good
news for us. Everything will be illuminated in the presence
of His glory. When you spend time in the glory, expect to be
shown areas where you need to change in order to allow the
gifts to truly flow.

*"My son, do not despise the chastening of the Lord, nor
detest His correction; For whom the Lord loves He*

corrects, just as a father the son in whom he delights." (Proverbs 3:11-12)

The discipline and correction of the Lord are actually good news. He does these things because He loves you. If you are not being chastened, you are not a true child of Father God. The writer of Hebrews knew this very well, and quoted this passage in chapter three of his book. Then he writes, *"If you endure chastening, God deals with you as with sons; for what son is there whom a father does not chasten? But if you are without chastening, of which all have become partakers, then you are illegitimate and not sons."* (Hebrews 12:7-8) These are all lessons we learn in the glory. Remember: Some things can only be taught in the glory. If you are struggling with this teaching, get into the glory and let the Lord reveal it to you.

ONLY AS MUCH AS YOUR LOVE CAN CARRY

"Pursue love, and desire spiritual gifts, but especially that you may prophesy." (1 Corinthians 14:1)

Have you ever met someone who seemed to be filled with anger and strife? After spending a little time with them, have you wanted to thank the Lord that they don't have much power to go with all their bitterness? God only gives you as many gifts and as much power as your love can handle. Otherwise, you would be very dangerous to yourself and others. If you want more gifts and more power, the key is to seek more love. I am not talking about asking the Father to love you more. He already loves you with the same love He has for Jesus. What I am suggesting is that you ask Him to gift you to love others as He loves them. When you are able to do this, He can trust you with more spiritual gifts.

> *"A new commandment I give to you, that you love one another; as I have loved you, that you also love one another. By this all will know that you are My disciples, if you have love for one another."* (John 13:34-35)

This is not merely a suggestion so that we can learn to be happier together. This is a commandment given by the Lord Himself. This may be the area of our greatest failure as the body of Christ. There are too many angry Christians spouting out vicious words of judgment and condemnation. This is our worst witness to the world. It is by our love that the world will know that we are disciples of Jesus Christ. It is not by the correctness of our doctrine or the way we attack people we think are heretics. It is by our love.

I have been praying constantly for a time of great victory for the church as the gospel is spread around the world. But, something is holding it back. I don't believe that the enemy has the power to do this. I don't think that political groups filled with hate can do this. It is the lack of love which is holding us back. We need to spend more time in the glory and allow it to transform us. We need to allow our minds to be renewed by the Holy Spirit. You cannot host the glory if you are filled with anger, bitterness, un-forgiveness and strife. It will not happen. Consider again what Jesus said:

> *"Jesus answered and said to him, "If anyone loves Me, he will keep My word; and My Father will love him, and We will come to him and make Our home with him. He who does not love Me does not keep My words; and the word which you hear is not Mine but the Father's who sent Me."* (John 14:23-24)

Jesus made it very plain so that we could not avoid understanding His meaning. You are either obedient or disobedient. If you don't love, you are not obedient, and you will not have the

Father coming to dwell in you. Without obedience you cannot host the glory or carry the gifts and the power. Now, is the time to pursue love with more intensity than you have ever sought it in the past. It is time for us to become the obedient body of Christ and to start loving others as He has loved us. How can we do that? The Lord did not leave us without resources. Study the passage below and seek the help of the Holy Spirit to receive wisdom and revelation to fully grasp it and live by it. Remember that the Helper is no longer on the way. He is here now!

"These things I have spoken to you while being present with you. But the Helper, the Holy Spirit, whom the Father will send in My name, He will teach you all things, and bring to your remembrance all things that I said to you. Peace I leave with you, My peace I give to you; not as the world gives do I give to you. Let not your heart be troubled, neither let it be afraid." (John 14:25-27)

PRAYER

"Father, I desire that they also whom You gave Me may be with Me where I am, that they may behold My glory which You have given Me; for You loved Me before the foundation of the world. O righteous Father! The world has not known You, but I have known You; and these have known that You sent Me. And I have declared to them Your name, and will declare it, that the love with which You loved Me may be in them, and I in them." (John 17:24-26)

SELAH QUESTIONS

1. How does the glory move us beyond ourselves?

2. In what ways has the glory made you fruitful?

3. How are spiritual gifts imparted?

4. What are some of the spiritual gifts the Holy Spirit has given to you?

5. Do you have enough love to carry more gifts and more power?

6. What are some of the ways to get more of the Father's love?

CHAPTER 13

LEVEL 4: THE JOY GLORY

One of the best examples of the "Joy Level of Glory" was seen in several of the revivals and outpourings in the latter part of the past century. These manifestations came as a startling surprise to many people. Some welcomed and embraced them, while others spoke very strongly against these manifestations. Since that time, we have personally experienced this level of glory manifest quite frequently in our meetings. Instead of surprise, we welcome it with heartfelt gratitude. In this level of the glory, we have seen many people receive inner healing and get set free from worry, anxiety, stress, and fear! In the joyous blessing flow of this level of glory, the power of God is released to set His children free. Demonic oppression is broken off and spirits of depression are bound and cast out by the Holy Spirit when this level of glory manifests. No work of man is necessary for deliverance when the Spirit of glory is present and at work. When this happens, all of the glory belongs to the Lord.

It seems odd that people who claim to believe in the Bible would be surprised by the appearance of these manifestations of joy. Joy is mentioned 150 times in the New King James Version of the Bible and 213 times in the New International Version. John tells us that joy is the motivation behind the writing of his first letter: "*And these things we write to you that your joy may be full.*" Jesus gave the same reason for His ministry of teaching the disciples: "*These things I have spoken to you, that My joy may remain in you, and that your joy may be full.*" (John 15:11) Based on this, I came to the conclusion that it is very important to the Lord for us to hear and preach the Word of God so that our "*joy may be full.*"

I really like this idea of the fullness of joy. I want my joy to be full! How about you? I also want your joy to be full, and that is one of the reasons why I am writing these things for you. Are you ready to receive it? Are you ready to live in the fullness of joy? If it bothers you to be so full of joy that you roll on the floor laughing, you may not yet be ready for this level of fullness being released by the Holy Spirit. One of the very interesting things about the joy glory is that it tends to rid us of pride as it sets us free from the power of the spirit of religion. It seems pretty undignified to the religious spirit for us to be on the floor rolling with joy and laughter. The religious spirit does not want to see people collapsed in chairs expressing the depth of their newfound joy with boisterous laughter. I just have one thing to say about that. I will use the words David used when he dealt with his bitter and fruitless wife: "*And I will be even more undignified than this, and will be humble in my own sight.* Think about this as you read that account again. Are you willing to be undignified in front of people in order to remain humble before the Lord?

> "*So David said to Michal, 'It was before the Lord, who chose me instead of your father and all his house, to appoint me ruler over the people of the Lord, over Israel. Therefore I will play music before the Lord. And I will be even more undignified than this, and will be humble in my own sight. But as for the maidservants of whom you have spoken, by them I will be held in honor.' Therefore Michal the daughter of Saul had no children to the day of her death.*" (2 Samuel 6:21-23)

Michal brought a curse upon herself by criticizing a joy filled outpouring of pure worship for the Lord. I wonder how many of us may be unfruitful for the same reason. If you want to release the gifts and the power, you need to get caught up in the joy of the Lord. Paul makes a strong statement about the connection between joy and glory in 1 Thessalonians 2:20, *"For you are our glory and joy."* Nehemiah spoke a similar word over the people on the day Ezra the Priest stood on the Temple Mount and read the Torah. *"Then he said to them, "Go your way, eat the fat, drink the sweet, and send portions to those for whom nothing is prepared; for this day is holy to our Lord. Do not sorrow, for the joy of the Lord is your strength."* (Nehemiah 8:10) It is important to remember that the joy of the Lord is not a weakness. It is your strength.

Peter also made a strong connection between joy and glory in his first letter. As he described it, he spoke of a joy which is both inexpressible and full of glory. How would you like to be so full of joy that you couldn't put all of your wonderful feelings into words? How would you like to experience the fullness of the glory in a mighty outpouring of deep joy? There is something very powerful about the joy of the Lord which breaks us free from every oppressive spirit and lifts us to new levels of His glory. I don't know about you, but I want more of it!

> *"In this you greatly rejoice, though now for a little while, if need be, you have been grieved by various trials, that the genuineness of your faith, being much more precious than gold that perishes, though it is tested by fire, may be found to praise, honor, and glory at the revelation of Jesus Christ, whom having not seen you love. Though now you do not see Him, yet believing, you rejoice with joy inexpressible and full of glory, receiving the end of your faith—the salvation of your souls."* (1 Peter 1:6-9)

We have been experiencing this level of joy more and more in recent outpourings of the glory. Dignified people dressed to perfection are suddenly so filled with joy that they are overcome by it. We have seen it in churches large and small. We have seen it in Theological Seminaries in the middle of their meetings. Often those filled with joy just fall to the floor and roll around with uncontrollable laughter. Sometimes they fall back in their seats and let the joy be expressed in loud and extended laughter. We have even seen it manifest in cafeterias as people share their testimonies of what the Lord is doing for them. Joy is breaking out everywhere! Hallelujah!

JOY IS SOMETHING YOU CAN ENTER INTO

"His lord said to him, 'Well done, good and faithful servant; you were faithful over a few things, I will make you ruler over many things. Enter into the joy of your lord.'" (Matthew 25:21, and 23)

Consider carefully what Jesus said in these two identical passages. You can enter into this level of the Lord's glory. You can seemingly just step into it. I pray that the Lord will bring everyone to the place where He can release His glory and fill them with joy and laughter. I am praying for a double portion of the joy of the Lord. How about you? I love it when this anointing falls on people; especially for those who seem to have little or no joy. I love to see it happen to people who have been very critical about it, because I then know that they have been set free from the oppression of the religious spirit. I love to see people who suddenly get filled and overcome by the joy of the Lord.

Being in the presence of the Lord's glory is one of the greatest joys you can experience. I don't think you can be in a glory outpouring and fail to experience it as a joy outpouring. If you are not experiencing it, perhaps you need to press in for it. Ask and you shall receive. We all need to persistently go before the

Lord with these requests on our heart. We can confidently do this because we know and understand that when the joy of the Lord manifests in our lives it brings glory to the Father, the Son, and the Holy Spirit.

"You will show me the path of life; In Your presence is fullness of joy; At Your right hand are pleasures forevermore." (Psalm 16:11)

JOY IS A SOURCE OF PERSISTENCE

"Therefore we also, since we are surrounded by so great a cloud of witnesses, let us lay aside every weight, and the sin which so easily ensnares us, and let us run with endurance the race that is set before us, looking unto Jesus, the author and finisher of our faith, who for the joy that was set before Him endured the cross, despising the shame, and has sat down at the right hand of the throne of God." (Hebrews 12:1-2)

The writer of the book of Hebrews says that it was the joy which the Father set before Him which enabled Jesus to endure the cross and the shame attached to it. On my own, I would not immediately associate joy with the pain of the cross. For me it is still an amazing thought that joy from the Father can give you the persistence needed to face anything–even something as painful as the cross. Jesus had to endure so much pain, suffering, and shame in order to accomplish our salvation, and it is important for us to understand what kept Him going through it all. This joy, which the Father set before Him, did something else which is very amazing. We learn in Hebrews Chapter 12 that it enabled Jesus to sit down at the *"right hand of the throne of God."* Having this kind of joy is another key to open Heaven so that you can visit the throne of grace.

One of the facts of this current season of spiritual warfare is that there will be times of pain and suffering. We will have to endure seasons of hardship, and we need something to sustain us during these times. What will sustain you? Some people have been misled into believing that if they accept Christ as their savior their troubles will be over. This is simply not true. When these people face hardships and challenges they either believe that it is their fault because of some personal failure or that the gospel is false. Mature Christians know that hard times may come, but the victory has already been won. They know that they are more than conquerors in Christ Jesus. They are not surprised by the trials they face. Peter knew this all too well when he wrote:

"Beloved, do not think it strange concerning the fiery trial which is to try you, as though some strange thing happened to you; but rejoice to the extent that you partake of Christ's sufferings, that when His glory is revealed, you may also be glad with exceeding joy." (1 Peter 4:12-13)

Don't think it is strange that you face these trials, but also keep a kingdom perspective. When you are allowed the great privilege of partaking in Christ's sufferings, you can rejoice because you know a great secret. The battle has already been won, and when His glory is revealed, you are going to experience *"exceeding joy."* When grasped and held on to by faith, this knowledge can sustain you through every hardship and every challenge. In fact, you are free right now to receive and embrace that joy. I receive it by faith and give the Lord thanks and praise for it! How about you?

JOY IS A SOURCE OF STRENGTH

"And you became followers of us and of the Lord, having received the word in much affliction, with joy of the Holy Spirit," (1 Thessalonians 1:6)

Have you been going through a time of heavy affliction? Do you know others who have been living under very difficult circumstances? Have you grown weary and wondered if you have the strength to go on? If so, there is good news for you and for them. When you receive the Lord in these hard times, you are rewarded with an outpouring of the Holy Spirit which comes with great joy. The Joy level of Glory brings renewed strength in times of weakness. Sadness and heaviness can weigh you down, steal your energy, and destroy your effectiveness for the Kingdom. However, when the Joy of the Lord comes, your strength will be renewed. You will have new energy, new enthusiasm, new hope, and a new direction. Look again at Nehemiah 8:10 and think of all the ways the joy of the Lord has provided you with strength.

Do not allow yourself to be overcome with sorrow. This is not from the Lord. In the days of Nehemiah, some of the people looked at their circumstances and went into grief, because they were remembering a time when it seemed better. They were too bitter to allow themselves to become better. Nehemiah looked at things in a different way. He saw the possibilities of how it could be with the Lord's help. He looked forward to a day when the Temple and the nation would be restored and lifted up to a greater glory. With His eyes fixed on the Lord and what He could do, Nehemiah had his heart filled with the joy of the Lord. He wanted everyone to feel it, but some couldn't see beyond their circumstances. How about you? Will you be held back by only looking at what you have? Or, will you be filled with joy by seeing what the Lord is about to release into your life? Your choice makes all the difference in the world. How can the Lord give the fullness of His joy and glory to bitter, hopeless, depressed, and broken people?

JOY IS A SOURCE OF HOPE

"Now may the God of hope fill you with all joy and peace in believing, that you may abound in hope by the power of the Holy Spirit." (Romans 15:13)

I really like this passage from the book of Romans. Paul recognizes that the most important things we need in our current circumstances are joy and peace. For him, it seems clear that this filling with joy precedes the outpouring of hope. The human way is to go for hope first. Then you can express joy after you are able to find hope. But, it doesn't work that way in the spiritual realm. Go for the joy and peace first and then let hope follow.

Notice that hope comes by the power of the Holy Spirit and not by our positive attitude or self-comforting words. We don't build it up in ourselves so that we can take credit for it. Hope is a gift of the Holy Spirit which comes by His power. But, first he releases the joy and the peace. The logic of the world just doesn't work in the realm of the spirit and we need to accept that fact. If we will quit resisting and begin to do it God's way, things will get better much faster. What do you think?

"Now to Him who is able to keep you from stumbling, and to present you faultless before the presence of His glory with exceeding joy, To God our Savior, Who alone is wise, be glory and majesty, dominion and power, both now and forever. Amen. (Jude 1:24-25)

JOY IS A GIFT OF THE HOLY SPIRIT

"You became imitators of us and of the Lord; in spite of severe suffering, you welcomed the message with the joy given by the Holy Spirit." (1 Thessalonians 1:6, NIV)

216

There are many people who seem incapable of doing this. When they are suffering, the thing they need the most is the very thing they are unwilling to receive. They have become imitators of the world rather than imitators of the Lord. Paul is calling us to get back into the practice of doing things God's way. First receive the Word and welcome the message of the gospel. Then allow the Holy Spirit to release an outpouring of His joy over you and through you.

The challenge seems to be one of developing a kingdom of God focus rather than a natural world view. It has to do with developing and embracing a Biblical world view as opposed to a political or economic world view. The vital ingredients for sustaining the kingdom of God are not the same as those for the flesh. Paul points out something which seems very obvious. The flesh must be sustained by eating and drinking. We can all understand that food is necessary to maintain the life of our physical bodies. But, these are not the necessary nutrients for living in the kingdom of God. While we still feed the body, we keep our focus on the things which will sustain our spiritual life for eternity.

"Therefore do not let your good be spoken of as evil; for the kingdom of God is not eating and drinking, but righteousness and peace and joy in the Holy Spirit." (Romans 14:17)

Paul identifies three key nutrients for our spiritual well-being. Our need in the spirit is for righteousness, peace, and joy. All of these are supplied by the Holy Spirit. People today are very health conscious and this is a good thing. At the same time, you must be focused on nurturing the spirit which will outlive the body. What are you doing to keep your spirit well fed and hydrated properly? I am constantly seeking the bread of heaven, fresh oil, and the new wine of the kingdom to nourish my spirit.

JOY IS A FRUIT OF THE SPIRIT

"But the fruit of the Spirit is love, joy, peace, longsuffering, kindness, goodness, faithfulness, gentleness, self-control. Against such there is no law (Torah: teaching)." (Galatians 5:22-23)

I don't want my life to be summarized in the way David's wife, Michal, was described. She did not bear fruit during the remainder of her lifetime. Too many believers are living unfruitful lives. In giving a variety of surveys, I have found that many believers cannot identify even one person they have personally led to the Lord. After countless years of attending church and various social gatherings, they have not produced any fruit for the kingdom of God. This is tragic. We are called to work in the harvest fields, and we are expected to bear much fruit for the kingdom of God. Listen to what Jesus says about bearing fruit.

"Abide in Me, and I in you. As the branch cannot bear fruit of itself, unless it abides in the vine, neither can you, unless you abide in Me. "I am the vine, you are the branches. He who abides in Me, and I in him, bears much fruit; for without Me you can do nothing. If anyone does not abide in Me, he is cast out as a branch and is withered; and they gather them and throw them into the fire, and they are burned." (John 15:4-6)

Branches which do not bear fruit are cast out, gathered up, and thrown into the fire. Many people do not believe this is true even though Jesus said it. They believe that once they say a prayer for salvation they are protected forever. They are holding on to a manmade doctrine for comfort rather than facing the truth of Jesus' teaching. This notion that they are somehow exempt from the requirement to be fruitful is not in line with what the

Bible teaches. We are held accountable for the presence or lack of fruit in our lives.

However, I want to focus more on the positive outcomes of a fruitful life. First and foremost, you will please, bless and glorify the Lord. This is a reward in and of itself. But it doesn't stop there. A fruitful life is also a joy filled life. I like that idea. Think of the joy you will feel when you consider all the people you led out of darkness into the light of the kingdom. Every lost soul returned to the Lord gives the occasion for joy to flow among the saints and the angels of Heaven. One day you will be able to participate in the heavenly celebration of lost souls being returned to the Lord. Imagine the joy of seeing the faces of those you personally led to a saving knowledge of the Lord.

"For you were once darkness, but now you are light in the Lord. Walk as children of light (for the fruit of the Spirit is in all goodness, righteousness, and truth), finding out what is acceptable to the Lord. And have no fellowship with the unfruitful works of darkness, but rather expose them." (Ephesians 5:8-11)

So many of the letters in the New Testament speak of the joy which comes from knowing that the people you have influenced are walking in the light, leading obedient lives, and bearing much fruit for the kingdom. This kind of joy builds on itself and produces more joy. It continues to increase with each new generation of those brought back to the Father through faith in His Son, Jesus Christ. I want this kind of joy. How about you? It can be yours if you begin to produce fruit for the kingdom of God. Go forth and be fruitful! Remember what Father God commanded, *"And as for you, be fruitful and multiply; bring forth abundantly in the earth and multiply in it."* (Genesis 9:7) He told this same thing to one generation after another as He released them into their destiny. Those who embraced their calling and followed the leadership of the Holy Spirit always experienced the joy of the Lord as their reward. I want you to have many powerful and life changing experiences in the joy level of His glory. Step into it as you pray the two Biblical prayers below:

PRAYER

"Now may the God of hope fill you with all joy and peace in believing, that you may abound in hope by the power of the Holy Spirit." (Romans 15:13)

"Now to Him who is able to keep you from stumbling, and to present you faultless before the presence of His glory with exceeding joy, to God our Savior, Who alone is wise, be glory and majesty, dominion and power, both now and forever. Amen." (Jude 1;24-25)

SELAH QUESTIONS

1. In what ways have you experienced the "joy of the Lord?"

2. What is the connection between joy and glory in the Word?

3. In what ways can you enter more fully into the joy of the Lord?

4. What should this joy produce in your life?

5. In what ways is joy a spiritual fruit in your ministry?

CHAPTER 14

LEVEL 5: THE SHALOM GLORY

L ast year something amazing happened for us in one of the glory outpourings in Korea. As we worshipped the Lord and cried out to see His glory, something fell over us which was not visible but felt like a misty cloud. It wasn't full of energy or fire like so many of our other experiences in the glory. It was something like a cloud of peace which released a strong sense of quiet and calmness deep into our spirits and souls. As it rested on us, we were suddenly rested in it. It felt like our bodies were being refreshed and replenished as they are during a period of deep sleep. Even though I was teaching and ministering with all my strength, it felt like I was at the same time being rested, refreshed, replenished, and renewed in spirit, soul, and body.

In my Spirit, I heard the Lord say, "This is the Shalom level of Glory!" I had never heard of the "Shalom level of Glory!" It was a new thought and a new challenge for me. One thing I was certain about: I liked it and I wanted more of it. I wanted to know how we had accessed or had been freely given entry into this amazing experience of His glory. My thoughts immediately went to Hebrews chapter four, and I began to understand some things about the "rest of the Lord" at a much deeper level than ever before. I began a new journey in my studies to get a deeper grasp of the full meaning of shalom.

UNDERSTANDING SHALOM

"Peace I leave with you, My peace I give to you; not as the world gives do I give to you. Let not your heart be troubled, neither let it be afraid." (John 14:27)

Jesus made a strong distinction between the kind of peace the world gives and what He was imparting to believers. When we think about Biblical peace, we must always remember that it is referring to His shalom. The peace the world gives is temporary, limited, and fragile. The peace of the world is easily broken and can come to an end instantly. Through the centuries, promises of world peace have often been the prelude to war. It is as if peace is given to placate people until all the fighting preparations are completed and victory is assured. The Lord does not give His shalom in the same way the world gives limited and temporary experiences of peace.

When the word shalom is translated simply as peace, it does not account for the depth of meaning inherent in this powerful concept. It is very important to understand that the Hebrew word shalom does not have a one word equivalent in English. The word shalom means so much more than peace. Its real meaning is better translated as fullness or completeness. It means that nothing is lacking or wanting for you in spirit, soul, or body. It speaks of you having everything you need and it refers to your ability to rest in the awareness of this reality. It is similar to the outcomes lifted up in John's prayer: *"Beloved, I pray that you may prosper in all things and be in health, just as your soul prospers."* (3 John 1:2)

It is this kind of shalom you will experience when the Lord covers you with His shalom glory. There is simply nothing like it anywhere else in the world. You are suddenly immersed in a cloud of wholeness. In this cloud every need is met, and it goes far beyond what you have ever asked or imagined. All anxiety, stress and fear seem to evaporate and float away from you and from all those around you. It is absolutely amazing to be so completely at peace and yet fully rested and strengthened to continue your work of ministry with no sense of fatigue. This is a powerful fulfillment of a very old promise.

> *"Therefore, since a promise remains of entering His rest, let us fear lest any of you seem to have come short of it. For indeed the gospel was preached to us as well as to them; but the word which they heard did not profit them, not being mixed with faith in those who heard it."*
> (Hebrews 4:1-2)

A few weeks after experiencing this outpouring of the "shalom glory of God," we were on a ministry outreach tour in Israel during wartime. While we were visiting the Holocaust Museum in Jerusalem, the sirens blasted a warning about incoming rockets. Many people around us became very fearful and some went into panic. We were sitting near a wall of plate glass windows and one woman urgently tried to get us to move away from the windows. While we were thinking about it, that cloud of shalom glory came over us again. We were absolutely filled with a sense of comfort, protection, safety, and peace. In the atmosphere of the Lord's shalom glory, we knew we had nothing to fear and we remained in that place until the all clear signal was given. I am not recommending you to throw caution to the wind and take mortal risks. I am sharing an amazing experience of shalom glory. The key is to follow the Holy Spirit and to know with certainty when you have nothing to fear.

THE SPIRIT OF GLORY RESTS ON YOU

> *"If you are reproached for the name of Christ, blessed are you, for the Spirit of glory and of God rests upon you. On their part He is blasphemed, but on your part He is glorified."* (1 Peter 4:14)

This experience of shalom glory is more than an emotional experience of peace. It is experienced when something very powerful comes to you in the person of "the Spirit of glory and of God." When this powerful Spirit of God comes to you, it literally rests on you and in you. You are rested in Him and His presence brings you to a much deeper level of faith and trust. When the Spirit of glory rests on you, it is very difficult to get upset about someone reproaching you. Their words hold no threat for you, and their anger cannot cause strife to emerge from the perfect shalom of God. The Spirit of glory and of God is one of the seven awesome and powerful Spirits of God.

"And I looked, and behold, in the midst of the throne and of the four living creatures, and in the midst of the elders, stood a Lamb as though it had been slain, having seven horns and seven eyes, which are the seven Spirits of God sent out into all the earth." (Revelation 5:6)

Notice that all of these Spirits of God have been *"sent out into all the earth."* They are everywhere, and they are an ever present source of help, comfort, and peace for every Spirit filled believer. When we speak about an outpouring of the glory, we are talking about an amazing experience of the weighty presence of this Spirit. When you are caught up in this Spirit, you are filled to overflowing with the shalom of God. In this atmosphere, the Lord pours out many wonderful gifts to His people. My experience has been that one powerful part of these outpourings from the Holy Spirit is a download of revelation knowledge.

THREE UNEXPECTED REVELATIONS

"Now may the God of peace who brought up our Lord Jesus from the dead, that great Shepherd of the sheep, through the blood of the everlasting covenant, make you complete in every good work to do His will, working in

225

you what is well pleasing in His sight, through Jesus Christ, to whom be glory forever and ever. Amen." (Hebrews 13:20-21)

This is an amazing passage of Scripture with some hidden prophecy about the Shalom Level of Glory. The Father is working in each level of glory to make you complete, and this is the very essence of the concept of shalom. This is not something which can be explained simply as angels sent to minister to your needs. It is about the presence of the Spirit of Christ coming to you and resting over you. It is about the weighty presence of Almighty God filling His Temple in your heart. It is about the Spirit of glory becoming powerfully real in your life and ministry.

When the glory manifests, we must keep our focus on the Lord and what He is doing in our lives. As you experience the glory of God, angels accompany Him as He comes to you. A myriad of angels are always surrounding Him and doing His bidding. These angels are often released to do some amazing miracles, signs and wonders in your midst, but they never distract you from keeping your eyes fixed on Jesus. Their mission is to get your eyes back on the author and finisher of your faith. Their mission is to make Father God real in your life and in all your testimonies. This was the first powerful revelation released in the glory.

The second revelation comes after you have been lifted up into a new level of glory. We learned by experience and by a direct revelation from the Holy Spirit that once you have been lifted to a new level of the glory, you have access to that level as an ongoing blessing from the Father. The Lord gave us several amazing experiences of this truth to confirm the revelation. I shared above one example of being able to enter the "shalom glory" during the rocket attack in Israel. This was just one of many confirming experiences. Over and over this "shalom glory" fell on us during times of ministry and in times when we were reproached for our testimonies about Jesus and the manifestations of the glory of God. When the glory of God fell on us, it was always accompanied by healings, miracles, signs and wonders. When you have been elevated to a specific level of glory, you continue to have access to it through the ministry of the Spirit of glory and of God.

The third revelation was that each level of glory opens a new experience of working with the Seven Spirits of God. Powerful spiritual connections are made when there is an outpouring of the glory. Prophetic gifting is one example of how the Spirit of wisdom and revelation works in the glory. As I was thinking about these revelations which I received in the "shalom glory," I was reminded that this is also a work of one of the Seven Spirits of God – the Spirit of wisdom and revelation.

The Spirit of life is at work to strengthen you and build you up as you rest in His presence. The Spirit of truth releases fresh new things from the Lord and shatters the work of the spirit of falsehood. One constant experience in these glory outpourings is the powerful presence of the Spirit of holiness who is always accompanied by many angels of holiness who minister to assist people to become more separated from the world and separated unto God. The Spirit of Sonship manifests to release people from bondage to sin and death and then connects them with their amazing inheritance from the Lord. The Spirit of grace manifests to connect the bride of Christ to the bridegroom. It also releases people to experience the "great grace" and the "great power" which fell on all the believers in Acts 4:33. Would you like to experience these things? Ask and you shall receive! Amen? *"And let the peace (shalom) of God rule in your hearts, to which also you were called in one body; and be thankful."* (Colossians 3:15)

ANXIETY FREE LIVING

"Be anxious for nothing, but in everything by prayer and supplication, with thanksgiving, let your requests be made

known to God; and the peace of God, which surpasses all understanding, will guard your hearts and minds through Christ Jesus." (Philippians 4:6-7)

Have you ever advised someone to stop feeling anxiety, worry, and stress? Do you remember how they responded? They probably said something like: "That is easier said than done." Perhaps they answered back with something much less calm than that. You simply cannot talk yourself or anyone else out of anxiety and fear. There is a demonic spirit behind these feelings and it is very persistent. Remember what Paul taught in 2 Timothy 1:7, *"For God has not given us a spirit of fear, but of power and of love and of a sound mind."* People need to be delivered from these demonic oppressions. They need the help of God to be set free.

In the glory, we have seen many people set free from fear and anxiety by the power of God. During these experiences there was no deliverance ministry done by people who had to labor and struggle against the enemy. It was solely done by the power of God which accompanies His glory. This is especially true for those who enter into the Shalom Glory. Demonic spirits cannot do anything in the presence of the Spirit of glory. It is amazing and wonderful to watch the Holy Spirit minister to people at a deeper level than we can ever experience by our own efforts.

The Shalom Glory is literally an anxiety free zone. Enter into it often and keep yourself free. Always remember who is doing this: *"Therefore if the Son makes you free, you shall be free indeed."* (John 8:36) We are reminded once again to keep our eyes fixed on the Lord. He is the express image of the glory of God, and every experience in the glory serves to point our eyes and hearts back to Him. When you think of the Shalom of God, remember that Yeshua ha Messiach is the prince of Shalom. (Isaiah 9:6)

SPIRIT VERSION 2.0

"But above all these things put on love, which is the bond of perfection. And let the peace of God rule in your hearts, to which also you were called in one body; and be thankful." (Colossians 3:14-15)

As I was soaking in the Lord's presence, the Holy Spirit spoke something a little strange into my spirit. He said to write about: "Spirit Version 2.0" I thought that this must be given as some kind of high-tech response to this teaching. Think about it! We receive a new spirit when we are born again. This is Spirit Version 1.0. Are you with me so far? As I meditated on this, something strange was revealed to me. I saw something written very clearly which I was not able to find in the Bible. In the presence of the Lord, I saw a page which looked like it was from the Bible. My eyes went to one line which read: "Then the Lord will give him the Spirit of peace."

As I tried to understand this apart from the Scriptures, the Holy Spirit spoke into my spirit again about "Spirit, Version 2.0" At this point, I began to understand what was being revealed to me. At the new birth we receive a new spirit (new heart). Now in the Shalom Glory, the Lord is giving an upgrade to that spirit in the form of the "Spirit of peace (Shalom)" and this is "Spirit Version 2.0" This is the gift from God which keeps us in shalom and maintains our access to the Shalom Glory anytime we need it. It is what Paul called the peace which transcends our understanding. It is the peace that guards our hearts and minds to keep us in fellowship and a right relationship with the Father through Jesus Christ. Think on that as you study the passage below:

"Do not be anxious about anything, but in everything, by prayer and petition, with thanksgiving, present your requests to God. And the peace (shalom) of God, which

229

transcends all understanding, will guard your hearts and your minds in Christ Jesus." (Philippians 4:6-7, NIV)

PROSPERING IN THE SHALOM GLORY

It is important to note that this teaching is not just about financial gifts or acquiring wealth. Money is the lowest form of prosperity. Remember that we are to prosper in body and soul first. Then the other forms of prosperity can flow from these gifts from the Lord. Shalom and prosperity are often connected in the Bible. David connected peace and prosperity in Psalm 122:6-7, *"Pray for the peace of Jerusalem: 'May they prosper who love you. Peace be within your walls, prosperity within your palaces.'"* There is a twofold meaning of the word peace in Psalm 37:11, "But *the meek shall inherit the earth, and shall delight themselves in the abundance of peace."*

Shalom is first the absence of strife and conflict. But, it also has to do with *"the abundance."* Shalom opens the floodgates of Heaven to pour out blessing and favor on us and all we do for the kingdom of God. Think about it! If you inherit the earth, you must surely be prosperous. I am always amazed to see people get angry and upset when you mention prosperity. It is as if a spirit of poverty has a strangle hold on the body of Christ. Why are we so fearful of the Bibles' teachings about prosperity? Perhaps a spirit of fear has been released which is at work to prevent us from teaching about something we have received from the Spirit as our inheritance from the Lord. Look again at 2 Timothy 1:7 and remember what to do with the spirit of fear.

It is this same fear and lack of faith which blocks us from receiving all the Lord has for us. The blessing and the favor of the Lord have always had a second witness through the prosperity given to the Lord's people. Abraham was very rich and he was called the friend of God. But, money was not the only witness. The seven-fold blessing the Lord spoke over him released prosperity in every area of his life: spirit, soul, and body.

How do you get this established in your life? You open up and receive it from the Lord. *"You will keep him in perfect peace* (shalom and fullness), *whose mind is stayed on You, because he trusts in You."* (Isaiah 26:3)

SHALOM IS A FRUIT OF THE SPIRIT

"But the fruit of the Spirit is love, joy, peace (shalom), longsuffering, kindness, goodness, faithfulness, gentleness, self-control. Against such there is no law." (Galatians 5:22-23)

Again we should view the fruit of the Spirit as being multi-dimensional. In the case of peace, shalom is a gift to us from the Father through the Holy Spirit. Then, it is produced in us and flows forth from us to others as a form of ministry. We receive it, we experience it, and then we produce it as part of our ministry in the kingdom of God. Shalom is always a self-perpetuating gift of the Holy Spirit. It reproduces itself and will increase more and more if we allow it to fully function in our spirits. *"Lord, You will establish peace (shalom) for us, for You have also done all our works in us."* (Isaiah 26:12)

Isaiah gives us a beautiful picture of the fullness of this gift from the Lord. He does not simply give shalom as a gift. He establishes it for us! Isn't that amazing! When we are in a right relationship with the Lord, His peace (shalom) is established in us and over us. *"The work of righteousness will be peace, and the effect of righteousness, quietness and assurance forever."* (Isaiah 32:17) If the Lord establishes something, who can bring it down? Of course, the answer is that no one can tear down what the Lord has built up. The enemy cannot steal it, kill it, or destroy it. Listen to what Paul taught about peace and the enemy: *"And the God of peace will crush Satan under your feet shortly."* (Romans 16:20)

SHALOM PRAYER

"And the Lord spoke to Moses, saying: 'Speak to Aaron and to his sons, saying, In this way you will bless the children of Israel, saying to them:

The Lord will bless you and He will keep you; The Lord will make His face to shine upon you and He will be gracious to you; The Lord will lift His countenance to you and He will establish shalom for you.

And this will put My name upon the children of Israel and I will bless them.'" (Numbers 6:22-27, ONMB)

SELAH QUESTIONS

1. Have you experienced the "shalom glory?" Describe what it was like for you!

2. What can you do to help the Spirit of glory and of God to rest on you?

3. In what ways is shalom like the English word peace?

4. In what ways does shalom differ from the English word peace?

5. How can the Shalom Glory set you free from anxiety and fear?

6. How has the Father's gift of Shalom prospered your life and ministry?

7. In what ways are you currently producing shalom as a fruit of the Spirit?

CHAPTER 15

LEVEL 6: THE INTIMACY GLORY

—◦◦◦—

"Now it came to pass, as He sat at the table with them, that He took bread, blessed and broke it, and gave it to them. Then their eyes were opened and they knew Him; and He vanished from their sight. And they said to one another, "Did not our heart burn within us while He talked with us on the road, and while He opened the Scriptures to us?" (Luke 24:30-32)

How is your walk with the Lord? Have you experienced times of intimacy with the Lord like these disciples who walked home with the risen Lord Jesus? Have you had moments like they described when your heart burned with the passion of that intimacy? If not, I pray that you will soon have an experience which goes beyond heart-warming to heart-burning. I don't want any community in the body of Christ to hear what He said to the church at Ephesus, *"Nevertheless I have this against you, that you have left your first love."* (Revelation 2:4) I pray that the entire body of Christ will soon experience an elevation to this level of passion for intimacy with the Lord once again.

These things will happen when true believers are elevated to the level of intimacy glory. This is a very high level in the glory, and too few people persist in their passion for the Lord long enough to reach it. My first experience of this level of glory

234

came during my first visit as an adult to the Third Heaven. When I stood with Jesus in Heaven, I was absolutely overwhelmed by His Presence. I stood in awe unable to move or speak. All I could think about was Him and how much I love Him. This happened again and again as I began to move in the intimacy level of His glory. I pray that if you have not yet experienced this that it will happen very soon. It is an awesome and wondrous experience in our spiritual walk with the Lord.

AN IMPORTANT POINT: I am not sharing these experiences with you because I think that I am somehow special. There is nothing special about me which is not also special about you. I believe the Lord chose me to have these experiences with Him and to write this book for that very reason. It was so that everyone can see and recognize that it is all about Him. It is His work from beginning to end. It does not happen for someone because they are special. It is because He is so awesome and is willing to spend time with insignificant people like you and me.

INTIMACY OF WALKING WITH THE LORD

"So all the days of Enoch were three hundred and sixty-five years. And Enoch walked with God; and he was not, for God took him." (Genesis 5:23-24)

As you go through a study of the first book of the Bible, you will read about many people who walked and talked with the Lord. Some people don't believe that this is possible any longer. However, because of my personal experiences in the Third Heaven with the Lord, I strongly disagree. This was God's plan for all of us when He created the world. In fact, the reason He allows us to go from "glory to glory" is to lift us back up into that image which is capable of having a deep and intimate relationship with Him.

As you study the Book of Genesis, notice all the people who had this level of intimacy with Him. Adam and Eve walked and talked with God in the Garden of Eden. There was even a special time set aside for these walks. They walked with Him *"in the cool of the day."* (Genesis 3:8) Father God spent a lot of time with Adam and Eve teaching them about life and helping them to fulfill their purpose in the garden. The Lord spoke this purpose into Adam and Eve's lives when He said, *"Be fruitful and multiply; fill the earth and subdue it; have dominion over the fish of the sea, over the birds of the air, and over every living thing that moves on the earth."* (Genesis 1:28)

Abraham talked with God many times, and they developed a deep and intimate relationship. Abraham trusted God, because he knew Him and had a wealth of experiences with Him. God also shared things with Abraham which He didn't share with others. Over time, they became very close and we are told in James 2:23, *"Abraham believed God, and it was accounted to him for righteousness. And he was called the friend of God."* How would you like for that to be your legacy? I would love to be known as *"the friend of God!"* How about you? That should inspire us to spend more time walking and talking with Him.

All of these relationships which men and women had with the Lord are very special and inspirational. Yet, there is still something even more special about the way one man walked with God. Enoch walked with God in such a deep level of intimacy that he somehow just bridged the gap between heaven and earth. Without going through the process of dying in the flesh, he just stepped into eternity. One day, he was no more on earth, because he stepped into heaven to permanently be in the Lord's presence. He loved the Lord that much, and the Lord took Him home in a totally unique way. How would you like to have that kind of experience with the Lord? I know that I would love that. To move into this level of glory, we need to spend more quality time walking and talking with the Lord.

JESUS IS THE IMAGE OF THE GLORY

Take a closer look at Paul's description of the process by which we move from glory to glory. Notice that the process is about a transformation in those who are allowed to go beyond the veil. When we are elevated up from glory to glory, it is into "*the same image.*" What image is Paul talking about when he says this?

> "*Nevertheless when one turns to the Lord, the veil is taken away. Now the Lord is the Spirit; and where the Spirit of the Lord is, there is liberty. But we all, with unveiled face, beholding as in a mirror the glory of the Lord, are being transformed into the same image from glory to glory, just as by the Spirit of the Lord.*" (2 Corinthians 3:16-18)

I believe it means two things. The most obvious conclusion is that we are being transformed into the image of the Lord. When the veil is lifted, we are enabled to see something in ourselves which looks a lot like what the disciples saw on the Mount of transfiguration. That is a pretty amazing thought! Think about it! What image do you consistently see when you look in a mirror. From mirror to mirror things in the background may be different, but one thing is constant –YOU! Paul is saying that you are beginning to look more and more like Jesus in the fullness of His glory.

This can only happen after the veil has been lifted, because two things happen at that time. First, you are enabled to see things you couldn't see before. And then it is possible to see things in you which were covered before. This is the second aspect of the concept of "the same image." You can begin to see yourself as God created you to be. You see how you were supposed to look before the fall in the garden.

Remember what the Lord told Philip. He said that when Philip saw Jesus he had seen the Father. Now, something like that has started to happen in you. When you and I look at you, we see Jesus. When we see Jesus we see the Father. We're all beginning to look like members of the family of God. This is one of the most amazing and awesome revelations in the Bible. Jesus was in the express image of the Father, and we are being transformed into the express image of Jesus. Jesus is "the brightness of His (Father God's) glory," and you and I are being transformed into the brightness of Jesus' glory. Read the passage below again with these things in mind. To really grasp this you must have the veil removed. I pray that the Father will remove it right now from your eyes. Before you study the passage, take a few moments to ask the Lord to lift the veil from your eyes.

"God, who at various times and in various ways spoke in time past to the fathers by the prophets, has in these last days spoken to us by His Son, whom He has appointed heir of all things, through whom also He made the worlds; who being the brightness of His glory and the express image of His person, and upholding all things by the word of His power, when He had by Himself purged our sins, sat down at the right hand of the Majesty on high," (Hebrews 1:1-3)

INTIMACHY OF TALKING WITH THE LORD

Another powerful experience in the intimacy level of glory is to talk with the Lord on a regular basis. I like to converse with Him all through the day. He is so real to me on a moment by moment basis that I talk with Him about most things. When good things happen, I try to immediately speak words of thanks aloud to the Lord. When things are difficult, I like to ask His help to better understand the situation and to know how to deal with the real issues – the issues which are important to Him and the Father. Can we really know Him this way? I am certain that we are supposed to know Him like this. He said, *"I am the good*

shepherd; and I know My sheep, and am known by My own."
(John 10:14) He knows us and He expects us to know Him.
Think about this as you study the passage below:

"My sheep hear My voice, and I know them, and they
follow Me. And I give them eternal life, and they shall
never perish; neither shall anyone snatch them out of My
hand. My Father, who has given them to Me, is greater
than all; and no one is able to snatch them out of My
Father's hand. I and My Father are one." (John 10:27-30)

Obviously, the Lord expects all of His sheep to hear His
voice. If you are not hearing His voice, you may want to find
out why. It is in the intimacy of talking with the Lord that He
releases that assurance of your salvation. He knows everything
about you and loves you anyway. When you develop this kind
of relationship with Him, you are bonded with Him for eternity,
and no one can steal you from the hand of the Father. Another
interesting thing happens to us. We are suddenly consumed by
a passion to draw others into this experience with the Lord.

"So, when you pray in your private prayer language, don't
hoard the experience for yourself. Pray for the insight and
ability to bring others into that intimacy." (1 Corinthians
14:13, TMSG)

VISITING IN THE THIRD HEAVEN

In the last few years, many people have reported experiences
of visits to the Third Heaven. This has caused some controversy
in the church. Many people do not believe this is possible for
disciples today and consider such stories heresy. Others believe
it was possible for Paul, but that this time has long past. What do
you believe? When you thoroughly examine this idea, I believe
that this is a fairly common experience for people who walked

closely with the Lord. Some of the Old Testament prophets describe experiences similar to what Paul is writing about, but didn't call it by the same name. John certainly experienced Third Heaven visits several times in writing the book of Revelation.

Why does this idea bother people so much? I have thought about this quite a bit since the Lord commanded me to make many of these visits. At first, I didn't want to talk about it with anyone because of the criticism I received. But the Lord insisted and I obeyed. I want to assure you that these visits do not tempt you to boast about them. Most of my visits have included times of discipline, correction, and admonishment. They are very humbling experiences, especially when the Lord instructs me to tell others about my personal need for correction. Think about this as you read Paul's description of his experience. He doesn't even want to admit that it was him who had this experience. I can certainly identify with him on this issue.

> *"It is doubtless not profitable for me to boast. I will come to visions and revelations of the Lord: I know a man in Christ who fourteen years ago—whether in the body I do not know, or whether out of the body I do not know, God knows—such a one was caught up to the third heaven. And I know such a man—whether in the body or out of the body I do not know, God knows—how he was caught up into Paradise and heard inexpressible words, which it is not lawful for a man to utter. Of such a one I will boast; yet of myself I will not boast, except in my infirmities."* (2 Corinthians 12:1-5)

I believe that these visits represent the highest level of the intimacy glory. When you visit in Heaven, you literally walk and talk with the Lord. You sense things about Him and about yourself that you didn't know before. You experience revelation about yourself at a deeper level than you have previously known. You build an awe and respect for Him that goes higher and deeper

240

with every visit. I have often meditated on the imperative in James 4:8, *"Draw near to God and He will draw near to you. Cleanse your hands, you sinners; and purify your hearts, you double-minded."*

On the one hand, it is so wonderful to draw close to Him. On the other hand, you become more aware than ever that you need to get your hands and heart cleansed and purified to stand in His presence. At first, that second part of James 4:8 sounded to me like a judgment to be received with dread. Then I recognized it as an act of pure love. The Lord wants us to be close with Him, and He knows exactly what we need to do in order to make it possible. He is letting us know what needs to be done. As I studied this passage, I was drawn back to the challenging questions posed in Psalm chapter twenty-four and the answers the psalmist gave.

"Who may ascend into the hill of the Lord? Or who may stand in His holy place? He who has clean hands and a pure heart, who has not lifted up his soul to an idol, nor sworn deceitfully. He shall receive blessing from the Lord, and righteousness from the God of his salvation. This is Jacob, the generation of those who seek Him, who seek Your face. Selah" (Psalm 24:3-6)

As I studied the passages from John and Psalm twenty-four, I experienced a real dilemma. I know a little bit about how to clean my hands. After visiting Israel a few times, I had a better understanding about the way this was practiced by those ascending Mount Zion to visit in the Temple. But, the challenging question was about how to cleanse my heart so that it would be pure enough to enter His presence. Then a wonderful and comforting revelation came to me. The Lord has already done this for you and for me. When He died on the cross, He provided all we need to have our hearts purified and our hands cleansed. All we have to do is accept it and live in gratitude for what He has done.

241

In the tribulation of these last days, we are going to need this kind of intimacy with the Lord. I believe that this is the real reason why He is giving these Third Heaven experiences to so many people. He is preparing us for the days ahead so that we will have the resources to survive in the "great tribulation." I believe that this is described very well in Stephen's brief Third Heaven visit while he was being stoned to death.

"When they heard these things they were cut to the heart, and they gnashed at him with their teeth. But he, being full of the Holy Spirit, gazed into heaven and saw the glory of God, and Jesus standing at the right hand of God, and said, 'Look! I see the heavens opened and the Son of Man standing at the right hand of God!'" (Acts 7:54-56)

Something really exciting is happening in the spiritual realm right now, and this is a season for us to draw near to God. It is a season to consider again the heart felt cry of the palmist: *"But it is good for me to draw near to God; I have put my trust in the Lord God, that I may declare all Your works."* (Psalm 73:28) As exciting as this season is, I believe that it is just the prelude for the next great move of God. I want to be ready for that move. How about you?

I am praying for the body of Christ to heed His words about returning soon. I am praying for the body of Christ to get busy preparing for His arrival. I want to hear Him say, *"You have a few names even in Sardis who have not defiled their garments; and they shall walk with Me in white, for they are worthy."* (Revelation 3:4) I don't want to hear what He said to the others from the church in Sardis.

"And to the angel of the church in Sardis write, 'These things says He who has the seven Spirits of God and the seven stars: "I know your works, that you have a name that you are alive, but you are dead. Be watchful, and

strengthen the things which remain, that are ready to die, for I have not found your works perfect before God." (Revelation 3:1-2)

I want as many of us as possible to be ready for His return. We can only do this by allowing Him to transform us from glory to glory *"into the same image."* How about you? Are you personally ready for Him to come and speak judgment to you? It is time to draw near to the Lord and experience Him drawing near to us. We need Him desperately in this hour. Even so, come quickly Lord Jesus!

"Their nobles shall be from among them, and their governor shall come from their midst; then I will cause him to draw near, and he shall approach Me; for who is this who pledged his heart to approach Me?' says the Lord. 'You shall be My people, and I will be your God."' (Jeremiah 30:21-22)

PRAYER

"Therefore, brethren, having boldness to enter the Holiest by the blood of Jesus, by a new and living way which He consecrated for us, through the veil, that is, His flesh, and having a High Priest over the house of God, let us draw near with a true heart in full assurance of faith, having our hearts sprinkled from an evil conscience and our bodies washed with pure water. Let us hold fast the confession of our hope without wavering, for He who promised is faithful. And let us consider one another in order to stir up love and good works, not forsaking the assembling of ourselves together, as is the manner of some, but exhorting one another, and so much the more as you see the Day approaching." (Hebrews 10:19-25)

243

SELAH QUESTIONS

1. What can you do to have a more intimate walk with the Lord?

2. Do you believe that you can hear His voice and be led by Him today? How is this working in your walk with Him?

3. What are some of your experiences with Third Heaven visits? How do you feel about them?

4. Why is intimacy with the Lord so important for believers today?

5. How do you prepare yourself better to walk and talk with the Lord?

CHAPTER 16

LEVEL 7: THE UNITY GLORY

—⦿—

"And the glory which You gave Me I have given them, that they may be one just as We are one: I in them, and You in Me; that they may be made perfect in one, and that the world may know that You have sent Me, and have loved them as You have loved Me." (John 17:22-23)

This is a very amazing passage from the Word of God. This is the level of glory which is the end state of our transformation. *"Therefore, if anyone is in Christ, he is a new creation; old things have passed away; behold, all things have become new."* (2 Corinthians 5:17) When we are restored into the image of God, we can experience this kind of unity with the Father, the Son, and the Holy Spirit. Are you ready to be made one with the Father and the Son? Unity was the ultimate goal of Jesus' ministry. This is what Paul was writing about in 2 Corinthians 5:18-19:

"Now all things are of God, who has reconciled us to Himself through Jesus Christ, and has given us the ministry of reconciliation, that is, that God was in Christ reconciling the world to Himself, not imputing their trespasses to them, and has committed to us the word of reconciliation."

It is important to note that Jesus prayed for this several times. It is obviously very important to Him just as it is important to the Father. It was His very sincere desire for the disciples to live in this level of glory as they carried on His mission in the world. The legacy He left for them and for us was this unity and love. It is also important to note again that Jesus prayed this for you and me as well as the believers with Him at the time. Study the prayers of Jesus again with the knowledge of His plan and purpose during His ministry on the earth. As his time came to a close, Jesus was seeking the Father's help to make the effect of His sacrifice permanent.

> *"I do not pray for these alone, but also for those who will believe in Me through their word; that they all may be one, as You, Father, are in Me, and I in You; that they also may be one in Us, that the world may believe that You sent Me."* (John 17:20-21)

As I studied the prayers of Jesus, several questions came into my mind? I am sharing some of these questions with you so that you can seek the answers which will help guide you on your journey from glory to glory. How are we to walk in the fullness of what the Lord prayed? When we consider what He has done for us, how should that influence the way we live and work in the kingdom of God? How can we live in a way that honors this great sacrifice which was made on our behalf by our Lord Jesus?

> *"I, therefore, the prisoner of the Lord, beseech you to walk worthy of the calling with which you were called, with all lowliness and gentleness, with longsuffering, bearing with one another in love, endeavoring to keep the unity of the Spirit in the bond of peace. There is one body and one Spirit, just as you were called in one hope of your calling; one Lord, one faith, one baptism; one God and Father of all, who is above all, and through all, and in you all."* (Ephesians 4:1-6)

One of the most powerful challenges given to us is to walk worthy of our calling. As I thought about this, some additional questions arose. How can we do that? What will it look like when it happens? Can we ever actually be worthy of our calling? As I wrestled with these questions, it became clear to me that unity and love for others are the primary ways in which we can walk worthy of our calling. When we walk as Jesus walked, we will fulfill His plan and desire for our lives. At the same time, I am very aware that the true nature of our worthiness is what Jesus has imparted to us by what He did.

"And you, who once were alienated and enemies in your mind by wicked works, yet now He has reconciled in the body of His flesh through death, to present you holy, and blameless, and above reproach in His sight..." (Colossians 1:21-22)

We see so little of the spirit of unity working in our world today. It seems at times that everyone is polarized around their own issues. Because of this, they are separated from everyone else around them. In families, we see spouses polarized and standing apart from one another. We see parents polarized from the values of their children. Political parties have become so polarized and filled with anger that few of the important issues of our day can be worked out with any kind of agreement. Ethnic groups and religious groups are separated by their values and fighting each other as if their goal is to destroy one another. Nations stand against nations and the world moves toward the brink of destruction.

The Biblical concept of unity must seem very odd for people today who have experienced so little of it? Many people cannot even imagine living in peace, harmony and unity. When we talk about it, many people seem to think that it is some kind of impossible utopian dream. When people read about it in the Word, it seems very other worldly, and many believe we will only see it in heaven. The truth is that there is something heavenly about unity. It is God's ultimate plan for eternity. David's description in the passage below makes it clear that it is almost beyond our ability to describe the power and effects of unity.

Behold, how good and how pleasant it is for brethren to dwell together in unity! It is like the precious oil upon the head, running down on the beard, the beard of Aaron, running down on the edge of his garments. It is like the dew of Hermon, descending upon the mountains of Zion; for there the Lord commanded the blessing—Life forevermore." (Psalm 133:1-3)

As I studied the meaning and purpose of unity in the Word, I discovered several interesting things. The first thing I noticed was that unity is the ultimate goal of the five-fold offices of ministry. The Holy Spirit has set people apart for these five offices in order to bring the church to the unity of their faith and of their knowledge of Christ as the Son of God. The next thing I noticed was that this unity draws us to the one perfect man, Jesus the Christ. When this happens, the body of Christ is raised up to the stature of the fullness of Christ. As you study the passage below, notice that all of this has to do with unity.

"And He Himself gave some to be apostles, some prophets, some evangelists, and some pastors and teachers, for the equipping of the saints for the work of ministry, for the edifying of the body of Christ, till we all come to the unity of the faith and of the knowledge of the Son of God, to a perfect man, to the measure of the stature of the fullness of Christ;" (Ephesians 4:11-13)

In the unity level of glory, all of these powerful outcomes begin to manifest as the fulfillment of Christ's purpose. He came to bring reconciliation on multiple levels. He came first and foremost to reconcile God and humanity. Then the ministry of reconciliation worked to unify individuals with one another. Next, those who follow Jesus are to take up this same ministry and begin to do their own part in the ministry of reconciliation. As we continue this work, we must never forget that the first and ultimate goal of this ministry is to reconcile each of us with Father God. Paul described something very similar to this level of reconciliation in the fourth chapter of Ephesians.

"Make every effort to keep the unity of the Spirit through the bond of peace. There is one body and one Spirit—just as you were called to one hope when you were called— one Lord, one faith, one baptism; one God and Father of all, who is over all and through all and in all." (Ephesians 4:3-6, NIV)

As Paul describes this level of glory, he makes reference to something he calls *"the bond of peace."* All things are to be unified in Christ and this bond of peace helps to wrap all the different levels of glory into this ultimate experience of unity with the Lord. Everything is "one" with everything else in the unity level of glory. The New Testament church had already started to experience this, but it was somehow lost over time. Now we are being lifted from glory to glory in order to get back into the unity Father God intends. Now is our time and this is our current task in the Spirit. May we get back to this level of glory and hold on to it until Christ returns!

ONE HEART–ONE MIND

On my first tour of duty in Korea, I had a wonderful chaplain assistant who was married and had brought his wife into country at their own expense. They were so much in love that they refused to be separated. They did everything together. At that time, it was popular and relatively inexpensive to have running suits tailor made. He and his wife purchased matching suits and had a logo designed just for them. They had asked for the logo to say, "Two Shall Become One." The tailor understood what they were trying to say and translated it in a slightly different way, but failed to mention this to them. When they wore the suits, they proudly told people what the logo said in Korean. One day a Korean woman heard this, and explained to me that it didn't really say "two shall become one." It actually said, "One Heart — One Mind." This struck a chord with me and I thought about it many times. I realized that the actual Korean words spoke of an equally high level of unity. This is exactly how Luke described the unity in the body of Christ in New Testament times.

> *"Now the multitude of those who believed were of one heart and one soul (mind); neither did anyone say that any of the things he possessed was his own, but they had all things in common. And with great power the apostles gave witness to the resurrection of the Lord Jesus. And great grace was upon them all. Nor was there anyone among them who lacked;"* (Acts 4:32-34a)

With amazing speed, the New Testament Church moved through all the seven levels of glory. By the fourth chapter of the Book of Acts, they were already operating at the unity level. The passage above, which was taken from that chapter, describes this level in very great detail. They were of one heart and one mind. No selfishness was seen because they had true and holy love for one another. They shared everything and there was no lack among them. As a result, the apostles were operating with *"great power"* and *"great grace"* was on all of them.

This did not happen by accident. The Lord didn't say, "Wow! I didn't see that coming!" It was His plan from the beginning. He had not hidden this from the prophets or the people. The coming of this level of glory had been prophesied long ago by

Jeremiah and Ezekiel. The Word of the Lord given through the prophet Ezekiel is amazingly accurate.

> *"Then I will give them one heart, and I will put a new spirit within them, and take the stony heart out of their flesh, and give them a heart of flesh, that they may walk in My statutes and keep My judgments and do them; and they shall be My people, and I will be their God."* (Ezekiel 11:19-20)

UNITY PLUS AGREEMENT (=) POWER

When the New Testament Church ascended to this level of glory, Luke testifies that they operated in "great grace" and with "great power." My spirit is so hungry for this level of glory. How about your spirit? So many people are asking to see more healings, miracles, signs and wonders. I wanted to know how we can cooperate with the Lord in order to get back to this level of power in our ministries. So, I began to seek wisdom and revelation from the Lord. Why do some churches operate in the power gifts of the Spirit while others do not?

As I have studied this question over the years, I believe that unity is the missing key in many churches. Without unity and agreement we will always be lacking in grace and power. When the early believers reached this level of glory, Luke says that there was *"no lack among them."* I think this meant a lot more than just financial resources, food and clothing. There was no lack of grace or in the power gifts of the Spirit. They had all that they needed in spirit, soul, and body in order to fulfill their destiny in the kingdom of God. It shouldn't be a mystery. Jesus taught about it over and over.

> *"Again I say to you that if two of you agree on earth concerning anything that they ask, it will be done for them by My Father in heaven. For where two or three are*

gathered together in My name, I am there in the midst of them." (Matthew 18:19-20)

If two or three can get together in the unity level of glory, they will be able to receive everything they ask in Jesus' name. It is important to fully understand this part of the promise. "In Jesus' name," means in accordance with who He is, what He is doing, and what He calls us to do. It is a higher level of unity, because we are lifted up into unity and agreement with Him. It is time for the unity level of glory to be restored in the body of Christ. Too many groups spend more time fighting each other than they spend fighting against the enemy. This must stop! We must be restored to unity if we are to live worthy of our calling! Paul gives us the high challenge of coming into "perfect unity." Are you ready for it?

"Therefore, as God's chosen people, holy and dearly loved, clothe yourselves with compassion, kindness, humility, gentleness and patience. Bear with each other and forgive whatever grievances you may have against one another. Forgive as the Lord forgave you. And over all these virtues put on love, which binds them all together in perfect unity." (Colossians 3:12-14, NIV)

Remember that in the beginning of this book, I wrote about the attributes of God being revealed at every level of glory. Now at this level, we are expected to be demonstrating those same attributes. Look again at the first sentence in the passage above. Doesn't that sound like Father God? Doesn't it sound like these believers have truly gone from glory to glory into the very image of the Father and into the image of how they were created? To accomplish this, we must forget about our grievances with one another. *"You are still worldly. For since there is jealousy and quarreling among you, are you not worldly? Are you not acting like mere men?"* (1 Corinthians 3:3, NIV)

252

Now is the time for you to begin to *"Forgive as the Lord forgave you."* There are no acceptable excuses for us to be in strife and motivated by jealousy. We have an urgent mission to prepare ourselves and the world for the return of Jesus. Time is far spent! Now is time for us to walk worthy of our calling and to heed and obey the words of Jesus and Paul's instructions: *"over all these virtues put on love,"* Love is another powerful key which can bind us together, and bring us to this level of unity in the glory. It is time to grow up as believers. It is time to grow up into the image of our Lord, Jesus Christ.

> *"Instead, speaking the truth in love, we will in all things grow up into him who is the Head, that is, Christ. From him the whole body, joined and held together by every supporting ligament, grows and builds itself up in love, as each part does its work."* (Ephesians 4:15-16, NIV)

In order to truly reach its God given destiny, the church must come into unity with Christ. This does not mean that He finally agrees to do our will and accomplish our vision and purpose. It means that we the church finally get the message deep in our spirits that we are called to get on board with Him and the mission Father God gave to Him. Paul adds to this concept of *"growing up into the image"* by making it clear that we are to *"grow up into him who is the Head, that is, Christ."* Christ is the force which brings us together, joins us to one another, and binds us in the same way ligaments bind the bones in our bodies.

This building up in love has a great purpose in the kingdom of God. The ultimate goal has not changed. God was in Christ reconciling the world to Himself, and the greatest task He has given to us will also bring the greatest glory to Him! This task is to bring the Jewish believers and the Gentile believers together in perfect unity and love. Christ himself modeled this for us. In Him we see the coming together of both God and man in *"one new man."* Now, He is calling us to be another kind of *"one new man.*" We are to be made into one new man—Jew and Gentile joined together with the Lord. This will be the fullness of unity.

The Lord first established this in Himself and then modeled it for us. He did this so that He could do the same miraculous work in us. Are you ready for this level of the unity glory? Study the passage below and ask the Spirit of truth to show you the part you are to play in this new movement of the Lord. Ask Him to lead you step by step and from glory to glory into the very image of Christ—the one new man.

> *"For He Himself is our peace, who has made both one, and has broken down the middle wall of separation, having abolished in His flesh the enmity, that is, the law of commandments contained in ordinances, so as to create in Himself one new man from the two, thus making peace, and that He might reconcile them both to God in one body through the cross, thereby putting to death the enmity. And He came and preached peace to you who were afar off and to those who were near. For through Him we both have access by one Spirit to the Father."* (Ephesians 2:14-19)

PRAYER

> *"May the God who gives endurance and encouragement give you a spirit of unity among yourselves as you follow Christ Jesus, so that with one heart and mouth you may glorify the God and Father of our Lord Jesus Christ. Accept one another, then, just as Christ accepted you, in order to bring praise to God. For I tell you that Christ has become a servant of the Jews on behalf of God's truth, to confirm the promises made to the patriarchs so that the Gentiles may glorify God for his mercy, as it is written: 'Therefore I will praise you among the Gentiles; I will sing hymns to your name."* (Romans 15:5-9, NIV)

SELAH QUESTIONS

1. In what ways have you experienced the same glory and the same love the Father gave to Jesus?

2. In what ways has your life reflected walking worthy of your calling?

3. What can you do to cooperate with the Lord in lifting you into the unity glory?

4. What do you need to do in order to rid yourself of the characteristics which block you from experiencing this level of glory?

5. What can you do to begin to demonstrate the same attributes as those you see in Father God?

SUMMARY

———❦———

"For the earth will be filled with the knowledge of the glory of the Lord, as the waters cover the sea." (Habakkuk 2:14)

The Word of the Lord given through Habakkuk is something to really get excited about. As I read it again, I began to try to visualize this. I immediately received a vision in which I was positioned far out in space looking at the earth from a long enough distance for it to appear like a globe. As I watched this beautiful blue planet created by our awesome Father God, I saw something like amber fire moving to cover the entire earth. It was not fire, but the glory of the Lord, and it covered the entire earth in an instant. Wow! That is an exciting thought and I am ready to see it manifest! How about you?

Then I was suddenly repositioned and placed on a small hill overlooking a beautiful valley with a peaceful little village in the distance. Suddenly the glory of the Lord coved the entire area in front of me like the waters covered the sea. This was very exciting for me, because I am truly addicted to the glory of the Lord. I am longingly looking forward to the fulfillment of the promise He released through the prophet Ezekiel.

"I will set My glory among the nations; all the nations shall see My judgment which I have executed, and My hand which I have laid on them." (Ezekiel 39:21)

I have a passion to personally witness the fulfillment of this promise, and I believe we are living in the days of its manifestation. I believe that this is why so many people are experiencing the glory in so many different places around the world. His glory is covering the earth right now. This is a season when we can all start to move with Him from glory to glory into the very image of Jesus and back into the image of our creator.

"For thus says the Lord of hosts: 'Once more (it is a little while) I will shake heaven and earth, the sea and dry land; and I will shake all nations, and they shall come to the Desire of All Nations, and I will fill this temple with glory,' says the Lord of hosts. 'The silver is Mine, and the gold is Mine,' says the Lord of hosts. 'The glory of this latter temple shall be greater than the former,' says the Lord of hosts. 'And in this place I will give peace,' says the Lord of hosts." (Haggai 2:6-9)

Are you ready for a little shaking from the Lord? I know that I am! It is time for Him to shake the heavens and the earth once more. He will shake some things off of all the world systems. Then He will shake the things of the Kingdom back into every place of governance in the world. This frightens some people because it means that many things are going to change. We will have to let go of the things we have been holding on to like security blankets in order to receive and move with the new things. The Lord gave me a vision about this earlier today. I am sharing it with you as I wrote it in my journal.

(A Vision To Help Us Let Go and Move Forward)

This morning the presence of the Lord was awesome and our worship room seemed to be supercharged with the power of His presence. We just soaked in and luxuriated in it for a long time as we sang praise songs. We truly experienced entering

His gates with thanksgiving. Then we entered His courts with praise and thanksgiving and it was awesome.

After a short period of time, I went face down on the floor and submitted myself completely to Him. After being in His presence for some time, I asked if there was a word to send forth today. As soon as I said that, I was carried by the Spirit to the outside of a very large building which looked like a warehouse. I was outside looking at the loading dock where one large truck was backed up to the dock. The driver was sitting in the cab of the truck with the door open as he waited for the loading process to be completed. I climbed up the steps to the dock and then went inside the warehouse. Many people were packing wooden pallets with packages of bread. I joined in and began to load the pallet assigned to me. Some of the packages looked like hamburger buns, some like hot dog buns, and some like various kinds of loaves of bread.

I heard someone suggest that we all stop loading the truck, and wait for people to eat all of the stale bread first so there would be no waste. This didn't seem quite right, but everyone paused to consider it. Then suddenly, the vision ended. I didn't really understand it so I asked the Lord to help me understand what it meant and to tell me if I should share this message. I didn't hear the Lord speak, but I was suddenly carried back to the area outside the loading dock and went through the entire process again.

This time, when the suggestion was made for us to wait until all of the stale bread had been eaten, the Lord spoke. He said, "The fresh bread will become stale while you wait. Then the people will receive more stale bread to eat before the next shipment. They will constantly receive and eat stale bread. Stop holding on to the stale bread! Let it go! Embrace the new bread! If you don't do this right away you will miss the new things I am releasing and remain unprepared for the new thing I am about to do!"

Did you receive it? I did! I started to think about the stale bread I have been eating and the things I have not been willing to let go of in order to accept the Lord's new things. One thing I know! I want to be part of the new thing the Lord is doing and I am ready to let go of everything that hinders. The Lord said, "If you release the fresh bread, people will be drawn to the sweet fragrance of the gospel. If you give out fresh bread the taste of the Bread of Heaven will go deep into their being." At this point I remembered and identified with what Paul taught in the third chapter of his letter to the Philippians.

"Not that I have already attained, or am already perfected; but I press on, that I may lay hold of that for which Christ Jesus has also laid hold of me. Brethren, I do not count myself to have apprehended; but one thing I do, forgetting those things which are behind and reaching forward to those things which are ahead, I press toward the goal for the prize of the upward call of God in Christ Jesus. Therefore let us, as many as are mature, have this mind; and if in anything you think otherwise, God will reveal even this to you. Nevertheless, to the degree that we have already attained, let us walk by the same rule, let us be of the same mind." (Philippians 3:12-16)

I pray that we will be enabled by the Lord to let go of the things which hinder us! I pray that we will press in toward the goal of our higher calling! I pray that we will develop a real taste for the fresh Bread of Heaven and seek it anew every day! May the Lord bless you with a deep hunger for His Word and a strong thirst for the living water which refreshes in spirit, soul, and body! Amen and Amen!

(End of the Vision)

We began to experience the glory coming into our meetings on a regular basis in the fall of 2011. Then in the Fall of 2012, I heard the Lord say over and over, "I will no longer share my glory with any man! I will no longer share my glory with any woman! I will do a new thing which is so new that you will not have a language to describe it! Then you will have no choice but to give me all the glory!" I like this word from the Lord. It is time for us to stop looking for the man or woman of God and begin to look to the God of men and women. It is time to look to the wise and holy God who is fully capable and ready to do new things. It is time to stop trying to take glory for ourselves and return it to the only one who really deserves it.

> *"Thus says the Lord: 'Let not the wise man glory in his wisdom, let not the mighty man glory in his might, nor let the rich man glory in his riches; But let him who glories glory in this, that he understands and knows Me, that I am the Lord, exercising loving-kindness, judgment, and righteousness in the earth. For in these I delight,' says the Lord."* (Jeremiah 9:23-24)

I want to do the things which delight the Lord. Every day I pray to know what we can do to please Him, bless Him and honor Him. Every day I am seeking ways to bring glory to the Lord. When we are fully committed to giving Him all the glory, something amazing begins to happen. His glory – the weighty presence – begins to manifest in our worship, in our conferences, and in our quiet times with Him. This is what I long for, and this is what I live for. How about you? Are you hungry and thirsty for more of Him?

My goal in writing this book was to assist you in finding ways to experience the glory of God more often and in exciting new ways. He does new things all the time. Don't expect Him to do it like you experienced Him before. This is good news because there is so much more of Him for us to experience. We can't see it all in one lifetime. I'm certain that we will not see and experience it all in eternity. That is exciting for me! I worship the God who declares, *"Behold, I make all things new!"* (Revelation 21:5) I am ready to be made new, and I pray that you are also ready for Him to take you from glory to glory and transform you into "the same image."

OTHER BOOKS BY THIS AUTHOR

"A Warrior's Guide to the Seven Spirits of God"–Part 1: Basic Training, by James A. Durham, Copyright © James A. Durham, printed by Xulon Press, August 2011.

"A Warrior's Guide to the Seven Spirits of God"–Part 2: Advanced Individual Training, by James A. Durham, Copyright © James A. Durham, printed by Xulon Press, August 2011.

"Beyond the Ancient Door"–Free to Move About the Heavens, by James A. Durham, Copyright © James A. Durham, printed by Xulon Press, April 2012.

"Restoring Foundations for Intercessor Warriors" by James A. Durham, Copyright © James A. Durham, printed by Xulon Press, May 2012.

"Gatekeepers Arise!" by James A. Durham, Copyright © James A. Durham, printed by Xulon Press, February 2013

CPSIA information can be obtained at www.ICGtesting.com
Printed in the USA
BVOW08s0034170714

359444BV00002B/2/P

9 781626 978294